Routledge Revivals

The Vertical Man

Originally published in 1947, *The Vertical Man* explores a form of Indian sculpture largely ignored in other studies, with a focus on two kinds of sculpture from the province of Bihar.

The book provides detailed analysis of the formal characteristics of the sculpture and the influences of the myth, ritual, and context in which they were commissioned and made. It explains why the sculpture is regional and "why the styles are what they are". It is an original study which throws light on important subjects, such as the relations between art and religion and art and economics.

The Vertical Man will appeal to those with an interest in art, specifically sculpture and the art of the Indian countryside.

The Vertical Man

A Study in Primitive Indian Sculpture

By W. G. Archer

First published in 1947
by George Allen & Unwin

This edition first published in 2020 by Routledge
2 Park Square, Milton Park, Abingdon, Oxon, OX14 4RN
and by Routledge
605 Third Avenue, New York, NY 10017

Routledge is an imprint of the Taylor & Francis Group, an informa business

© W. G. Archer 1947

All rights reserved. No part of this book may be reprinted or reproduced or utilised in any form or by any electronic, mechanical, or other means, now known or hereafter invented, including photocopying and recording, or in any information storage or retrieval system, without permission in writing from the publishers.

Publisher's Note
The publisher has gone to great lengths to ensure the quality of this reprint but points out that some imperfections in the original copies may be apparent.

Disclaimer
The publisher has made every effort to trace copyright holders and welcomes correspondence from those they have been unable to contact.

A Library of Congress record exists under LCCN: 48008430

ISBN 13: 978-0-367-61127-9 (hbk)
ISBN 13: 978-1-003-10424-7 (ebk)

CHAKANDHAWA

THE VERTICAL MAN

A STUDY IN PRIMITIVE INDIAN SCULPTURE

by

W. G. Archer

Special Edition For Sale
In India Only

London
George Allen & Unwin Ltd

FIRST PUBLISHED IN GREAT BRITAIN 1947

FIRST PUBLISHED IN INDIA 1947
540 copies

ALL RIGHTS RESERVED

Let us honour if we can
The vertical man
W. H. Auden

Art is a mathematics of the heart
D. V. Fumet

To
EDWARD WELBOURNE

PREFACE

IN a contribution to *The Painters' Object*,[1] John Piper made a brilliant preliminary analysis of certain styles of English medieval sculpture to which little attention has hitherto been paid. These styles are found mainly in English parish churches, in the isolation of the countryside, and they represent levels of English sensibility quite distinct from those which produced the main cathedral styles—the styles which we summarize as the Winchester, Canterbury, Durham and York schools of sculpture. Just as these schools stamped their styles on the wealthy products of certain areas, local peasant traditions produced their "county" styles—phrasing and formulating the more lowly sculpture of the village churches. Between the two types there is a gap—as rigid as that between two social classes, the townsman and the countryman, the squire and the peasant, the bishop and the country parson. The cathedral styles came from the floating culture of Western Europe—a culture which expressed "a gentle melodic sensibility." They spread wherever wealth could finance a cosmopolitan element but they did not percolate to the villages. The village styles, on the other hand, grew up in a cultural vacuum. They neither influenced the cathedrals nor were influenced by them—for the medieval town was far from the village and there was no critical consciousness to disturb the village way of carving. The cathedral styles are intellectual refinements of a semi-English sensibility. The peasant styles represent the English sensibility in its robust essentials.[2]

If we compare this position with the situation in India, we shall find a striking similarity. In India, as in England, there are two types of sculpture. The first which has hitherto defined Indian sculpture for the West is principally the sculpture of the larger temples. This sculpture moves between the religious

[1] Myfanwy Evans, ed., *The Painter's Object* (London, 1937), article by John Piper, "England's Early Sculptors," 117–125.

[2] Compare Herbert Read, "English Gothic," *The Listener*, May, 1930: "There existed all through the Gothic period the hieratic art of the church, tending towards symbolism, intellectuality, conventions of all kinds; but there also existed a subterranean art which was the art of the common people, vigorous, unlearned, even barbaric."

10   THE VERTICAL MAN

diagram and the literal portrait and although it expresses certain
values of ideal anatomy and indicates certain religious poses, it
is as little indicative of Indian sensibility as a whole as the cathedral
styles are summaries of English sculpture. As against this temple
carving, there is a series of regional peasant styles. These represent
a type of sensibility which in essentials is the same as that displayed
in early English churches. There is the same interest in abstract
rhythm and vital geometry and the same achievement of dignity
through formal distortions. A view which focussed on these
"subterranean" styles would find Indian sculpture strangely and
compulsively parallel to Negro and Celtic sculpture—a world of
art in which a contemporary mind can exult and delight.

In this book, I have taken two of these regional styles—styles
which are confined to the western portion of the Indian province
of Bihar and have treated the sculpture as *art*. That is to say, my
first concern has been with the formal values of the styles, the
impact of the images as works of art. But a study of sculpture,
particularly of a sculpture which is still in active production,
inevitably raises other issues, and I have used this contemporary
material to deal with such wider questions as the relations of art
and religion, the influence on art of economics—to attempt an
explanation of why the styles are what they are.

The basis of experience from which this book is written
should perhaps be stated. I first saw images of Bir Kuar in 1931
when I went with the late Mr. N. F. Peck, C.B.E., I.C.S., on a tour
for tiger in the Sasaram and Rohtas thanas of Shahabad. The
images with their brutal dignity excited me far more than any
tiger but it was not until 1935 that I was again able to go to the
area. In the winter of that year I went with Mildred Archer and
made a short tour of the Latehar subdivision of Palamau district.
This area lies north-west of Gumla in Ranchi district and is the
extreme western portion of the Uraon country. In this tour we
were only able to survey the fringes of the cult and I had again to
wait until 1938 before going to the heart of the region. From
October 1938 to February 1939, I made three sustained tours,
working slowly down the western and eastern sides of the Son
River, and visiting Ahir villages throughout the Sasaram subdivision of Shahabad and portions of Gaya, Palamau, Ranchi and
Hazaribagh districts. In these tours, I saw as many Ahirs as I

PREFACE 11

could, examined and photographed the sculpture, attended ritual and collected poems and legends.

Of the many who helped me at different stages during the last fifteen years, I am particularly indebted to Mr. E. T. Prideaux, O.B.E., I.C.S., and to Mr. M. Azfar, M.B.E., I.C.S., both of whom assisted me with their knowledge of the area, to Mr. M. I. Malik, Director, Veterinary Services, Bihar, for a note on buffaloes, and to Mr. L. R. Sabharwal, I.F.S., Conservator of Forests, Bihar, for statistics of tigers. My special thanks are due to Mildred Archer for constant stimulus and advice, to Rai Sahib N. L. Bhattacharjee for a map, and to Rai Bahadur Sadashiva Prasad for detailed and valuable criticism. I must also record my great indebtedness to Miss Beryl de Zoete for constructive suggestions. Above all, my thanks are due to Babu Sankta Prasad who not only shared with me the rigours of many journeys, but gave me continuous help in enquiries. But for his enthusiasm much of the preparation of this book would have been impossible.

W. G. ARCHER

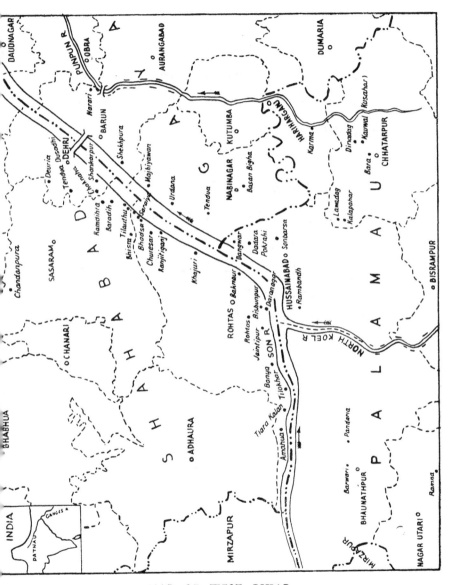

MAP OF WEST BIHAR

CONTENTS

		PAGE
	Preface	9
	Map of West Bihar	12
I.	Two Styles of Sculpture in West Bihar	17
II.	The Ritual of the Cattle-god	25
III.	The Myth of Bir Kuar	49
IV.	Wood and Stone	82
V.	The Region and the Styles	87
VI.	Why the Styles are what they are	91
	Appendixes	
	The Identity of Bir Kuar	99
	The Role of the Godlings	105
	The Control of Tigers	110
	Bibliographical Notes	113
	Glossary	115
	List of Villages	117
	Index	121

ILLUSTRATIONS

Images of Bir Kuar

Chakandhawa   *Frontispiece*

FIGURE

STONE

1 Khajuri
2 Ghuna Bigha
3 Chandanpura
4 Bhadsa
5 Dadara Pokrahi
6 Banua
7 Majhiyawan
8 Saraiya

between pages 16–17

9 Urdana
10 Tendua, Ratanpura tola
11 Daranagar
12 Bhisra
13 Tilokhar
14 Nishunpur
15 Baknaur
16 Dangwar

between pages 32–33

17 Tenua Dusadhi
18 Sheikhpura
19 Shankarpur
20 Baradih
21 Basant Bigha
22 Manhania
23 Amahua
24 Churesar

between pages 48–49

THE VERTICAL MAN

25 Tilauthu
26 Rohtas, Bholna tola
27 Ramdihra
28 Barka Tiara
29 Ramna

WOOD

30 Rambandh
31 Nimahat
32 Kusiara

between pages 64–65

33 Dinadag
34 Sonbarsa
35 Kusahar
36 Kalapahar
37 Rohtas, Bholna tola
38 Ramgarh
39 Ramgarh
40 Rohtas, Bhabhantalao tola

between pages 80–81

41 Ramgarh
42 Bara
43 Bara
44 Banwari
45 Pandaria
46 Jairagi
47 Jairagi
48 Karma, Bairia tola

between pages 96–97

1. KHAJURI

2. GHUNA BIGHA

3. CHANDANPURA

4. BHADSA

5. DADARA POKRAHI

6. BANUA

7. MAJHIYAWAN

8. SARAIYA

Chapter One

TWO STYLES OF SCULPTURE IN WEST BIHAR

I

IN the south-west corner of Bihar, the Grand Trunk road is both a highway and a frontier. To the north, beyond its metalled surface, lie enormous open fields, wide and bare, like the fens at Ely. To the south, the Son river swells to a great stream in the Rains—to expire in sandy flats as spring merges into summer. To the west, the tall cliffs of Rohtas loom, gaunt and grim, in the light of evening. The road is, as it were, the end of a civilization, for, as one travels south, the sense of safety ends. The flat lands merge in rough hills, the soil reddens, cultivation thins. One is in an area of tumbled and scraggy jungle, which ranges from dense and shaggy folds to stunted derelict uplands. In this jungle, the Ahirs graze their buffaloes, and through its wild and sombre stretches the tiger stalks.

Within this region each village has a form of stone or wooden sculpture. In places, stone and wooden images stand side by side. In others, wood alone is found, while in some the sole medium is stone. The latter marks the Sasaram, Dehri and Rohtas *thānās* of Shahabad, the Barun and Nabinagar *thānās* of Gaya and the Hussainabad *thānā* of Palamau, while the wooden figures flourish in Palamau district and in southern Sasaram. Each figure is normally made only for the Hindu caste of Kishnaut Ahirs, whose primary occupation is the tending of cows and buffaloes and its subject is their cattle-god, Bir Kuar. The stone sculpture is made by Gonrs, a subcaste of stone-cutters, while the images in wood are carved by Barhis, the caste of carpenters. No two figures are ever quite the same, yet the sculpture as a whole exhibits two distinct styles. Not only is each wooden figure related to a standard pattern, but the idioms of each image, its detailed ways of representing forms, are drawn from a regional stock. In a similar way, the stone images vary in details, yet, in basic conception, they, too, reflect a common style. It is, as it were, only in incidentals that an image expresses a particular

18   THE VERTICAL MAN

carver. Beyond the individual lies the community and the sculpture is, in fact, a clue to the needs and values of a region.

II

The basis of both styles is a will to what may be called vital geometry;[1] and before we examine them in detail, it is necessary to make clear exactly what we mean by this fundamental term. An art may be said to be geometric when it uses the abstract forms of geometry—the circle, the straight line, the square, and the angle; and a purely geometric art is one which is severely limited to these forms. Examples are paintings by Helion or the village paintings of Singhbhum Santals[2] in which the square of the picture is analysed into a series of subtly poised rectangles; or even certain plaques by Ben Nicholson in which the basic forms are circles and rectangles. In these kinds of art the forms are abstract in the sense that they correspond to certain mathematical concepts and do not derive directly from any vital forms. But even the purest geometry is not completely abstract for the presence of geometric forms in nature evokes human responses and charges them with vital associations. It is not true as Worringer thought, that "the rigid line is essentially abstract and alien to life" or that "the abstract geometrical line embodies no organic expression, no possibilities of organic interpretation."[3] The horizontal line is associated with the levels of a plain, the absence of obstacles, the recumbent, the passive and the female. The vertical line is linked to the thrust of trees, to energy, opposition, division, to the erect and the male. Similarly, the square and the triangle with their resolution into sharp points are associated with what is hard and brutal, the angular rock, the rational and masculine—the reverse of the curve with its yielding weakness, and feminine shrinkage.

[1] I have adapted this term from Herbert Read's phrase "vitalised geometry" in his translation of Wilhelm Worringer's *Form in Gothic*.

[2] I have discussed this type of painting in an article with Mildred Archer. (W. G. and M. Archer, "Santal Painting," *Axis* (London), Autumn 1936.)

[3] Wilhelm Worringer, *Form in Gothic* (transl. Herbert Read) (London 1927), 7 and 41.

TWO STYLES OF SCULPTURE IN WEST BIHAR 19

The vital associations of these forms could, in fact, be elaborated indefinitely. Worringer himself states, "What determines the impression made by the column is its roundness. This roundness at once evokes the illusion of organic vitality, because it directly reminds us of the roundness of those natural limbs which exercise a similar function of support, and more especially of the tree-trunk, which supports the crown and of the flower-stalk which bears the flower. Besides which, roundness in itself satisfies our natural organic feeling without the need of evoking analogous ideas. We cannot look at anything round without inwardly realizing the process which created that roundness. We feel above all the calm which evolves from this perpetual self-contained movement. The column, like the circle, is the highest symbol of self-contained and perfected organic life."[1]

Henry Moore has said, "It might seem from what I have said of shape and form that I regard them as ends in themselves. Far from it, I am very much aware that associational, psychological factors play a large part in sculpture. The meaning and significance of form itself probably depends on the countless associations of man's history. For example, rounded forms convey an idea of fruitfulness, maturity, probably because the earth, women's breasts, and most fruits are rounded, and these shapes are important because they have this background in our habits of perception."[2]

Even the most geometric art, therefore, is not entirely abstract and does, in fact, contain emotional over-tones.

Such an art, however, accounts for only a small proportion of sculpture and a far more common type may be termed semi-geometric and semi-vital. In this art there are two kinds and in both the starting-point is not with the abstract but with the vital. The artist takes the organic forms of the human or animal body and proceeds to distort them in the direction of geometry. But while in one class the geometry deadens, in the other it vitalizes. Where it deadens, the vital forms are distorted to make a geometric pattern which has no relation to their meaning. The pattern is, as it were, imposed upon them from outside—

[1] Worringer, op. cit., 91.
[2] Henry Moore, "Notes on Sculpture," *The Painter's Object*, 28–29.

THE VERTICAL MAN

as an automatic diagram—and the shapes lose their vitality in being absorbed by it.[1] In the other group the forms are given geometric distortions, but instead of a pattern being imposed upon them, as something alien and arbitrary, they are welded into a rhythm which is based on their vital functions. Equally, while the distortions simplify the forms in a geometric direction, they use the vital associations of geometry for intensifying their human power. The geometry also reduces the forms to a common denominator and so makes easier their fusion into a single compulsive whole. It is this latter type of art which we can properly designate as "vital geometry."

III

How then does the stone sculpture of West Bihar conform to this definition?

We have seen that the various images are distributed throughout the region and that, taken together, they express a regional style. When we subject this style to scrutiny, we find that a will to vital geometry is expressed in a number of distinct ways.

Firstly, the idioms or ways of representing the various human parts are given a geometric distortion. This is sometimes completely geometric and results in the pure forms of the circle or the rectangle. The head, for example, is treated as a circle,[2] the mouth, the eyebrows, the shoulders and the waist are straight horizontals,[3] the club is a straight line,[4] the eyes and ears are semi-circles,[5] the nose, the torso, and the legs are rectangles.[6] At other times, the distortion is partly geometric in the sense that the forms are almost but not entirely a circle or a square. In these cases, the geometric form is twisted in a vital direction and has both the severity of geometry and the appeal of the organic. The torso becomes a flat or tapering oval,[7] the arms are bulging semi-circles,[8] and the lines of the legs spring outwards in a rigid curve.[9] Finally, there are images in which the forms are vital rather than mathematical, but which yet contrive to

[1] Compare, for example, early Scandinavian fibulas and Southern Germanic clasps.
[2] Plates 13 and 23.   [3] Plate 14.   [4] Plates 4, 5 and 31.
[5] Plates 15 and 23.   [6] Plate 14.   [7] Plates 1 and 3.
[8] Plates 9, 10, 11 and 21.   [9] Plates 7 and 21.

TWO STYLES OF SCULPTURE IN WEST BIHAR 21

evoke a geometric tone. The arms and head are reduced to irregular curving forms,[1] or the arms, shoulders and club become a single violently twisting line.[2] In these images, the curves and angles are too vital to be regular but in their jagged simplicity they set up a geometric sympathy.

This will to vital geometry is similarly expressed in the rhythms. These are based on four geometric patterns—a vertical structure resembling a figure of eight,[3] a second somewhat similar pattern based on three ascending circles or ovals,[4] a third type based on interposing circles and rectangles[5] and, finally, an angular structure with a more horizontal movement based on two splaying diagonals.[6] These structures bear the same relation to the actual rhythms as a sonnet form or a blank verse form bears to the poem which uses it. They are fundamental frameworks on to which the idioms are fitted. But just as the process of writing a poem gives the verse form an organic irregularity, the process of carving the idioms modifies the structure. The rhythm of each image is not so much a mechanical repetition of a geometric structure as a vital organization of forms above it. The result is a system of rhythms and idioms which are geometric in their basic plan and tone but are otherwise fluid and vital.

IV

A similar effect is created by the wood sculpture but here the idioms and rhythms are somewhat different and there is an important respect in which the style in wood differs markedly from that in stone.

The style in stone is essentially linear. That is to say, the images are conceived as flat planes jutting from a flat background. The edges of these planes are sometimes angular and the images are then the exact equivalent of linear drawings. At other times the edges are rounded and the plane becomes less a flat expanse as a series of shallow globular masses. At no time, however, do the stone images become fully round. Their aim rather is to build

[1] Plates 25–27.   [2] Plates 12, 15 and 23.   [3] Plates 1–3.
[4] Plates 7 and 25.   [5] Plates 4 and 14.   [6] Plates 21 and 22.

22 THE VERTICAL MAN

up a flat geometric rhythm based on interposing lines and to reinforce it by the effect of light on slightly moulded linear forms.

In the style in wood, the sculpture is essentially round. The figure, instead of being posed against a flat plaque, becomes a separate tubular form. The head swells into a rotund globe, and while the arms and legs continue to be treated as almost entirely linear, the basis shifts from the flat to the round. The lines no longer fuse on a flat plane but develop their formal relations on the rounded surface of the tube.

Within these limits, the will to vital geometry employs two kinds of idioms. In the first the form is purely geometric and its characteristic shape is the vertical cylinder which represents the greater part of the body.[1] In the second type, on the other hand, the forms are no longer purely mathematical but retain a geometric simplicity. The arms, for example, are treated as curving lines which swing towards each other either in a smooth unbroken curve[2] or in one which is slightly angular and bent.[3] The fingers become slim and tiny rectangles which splay out from the wrists like a fan.[4] The legs, when they occur, are slightly irregular verticals.[5] The face is either a tapering oval, a rough circle, or a blunt rectangle and the features are never far from the austerity of the straight line or the rigid circular curve. Similarly, although the head is never a pure sphere or a pure cube, it has a suave and smooth simplicity, a rounded grace or an angular formality which links it to more purely geometric forms. The vital forms of the body are, as it were, injected with geometry and while they are never completely abstracted, their lines and masses are simplified into curving and angular forms with geometric tones.

Owing to the narrower range of the idioms there are fewer types of rhythm. The structure of one is a small oval poised on a larger oval and the rhythm consists in the swing of the lines round and across the curving masses of the cylinder and the head.[6] In a second the tubular form is divided into three dwindling sections, which are interlinked by the lines of the hair, eyes, mouth, hands and ribs.[7] Finally, in a type which is isolated from the others, the basic structure consists of two rectangles joined by a

[1] Plate 32.   [2] Plates 35 and 36.   [3] Plate 43.
[4] Plates 36 and 42.   [5] Plates 39 and 41.   [6] Plates 35 and 48.
[7] Plates 38 and 41.

TWO STYLES OF SCULPTURE IN WEST BIHAR 23

diamond-shaped parallelogram, and the rhythm is a system of balancing angles and rigid interfusing lines.[1]

V

But geometric rhythm is only one element in the two styles—the geometric in a will to vital geometry—and the same idioms and rhythms which produce an effect of mathematics are instrumental in projecting certain vital types.

The styles, while distorting vital forms in the direction of geometry, also distort their relative sizes and it is this which both contributes to a geometric rhythm and produces certain emotional effects. The enormous head on a stunted body,[2] the huge torso dominating the small head and legs,[3] the towering club,[4] the squat taut neck,[5] the massive thighs which dwarf the head and torso[6]—all these contrive to convey the sense of abnormal power. The human frame is not merely organized into a geometric scheme but becomes an image of a super-normal man.

The first of these summary supermen is a form which may be called the muscular guardian.[7] This type is presented through the following idioms. The use of heavy semi-circles and jagged angles for the arms and torso creates a sense of muscular brutality. The welding of the arms and torso into a single compact form gives them the effect of compressed energy. At the same time, the rigid line of the club concentrating the posture on a weapon, the strict circular lines of the head, the rigid horizontal line of the mouth and the downcast eyes show that a decision has been taken and that there can now be no weakening. The figure is, as it were, taut and braced for defence.

In the second type, the element of super-strength remains but the idioms create a type which may be called the benign hero.[8] The brutal angular idioms are discarded and circular distortions take their place. The curves have an element of gentle grace—an abstraction which is kindly rather than austere. The club is whittled down to a baton or is omitted altogether, and the

---

[1] Plates 46 and 47.   [2] Plates 3, 22 and 17.   [3] Plate 28.
[4] Plates 12, 15 and 16.   [5] Plate 20.   [6] Plate 7.
[7] Plates 13, 19 and 20.   [8] Plates 25, 33 and 37.

THE VERTICAL MAN

rotund head merges in the rubicund. It is as if the muscular hero is about to bless rather than to strike.

The third form may be designated the "doomed tough."[1] In these images, the sense of power is conveyed through the large over-loaded head or the swelling thighs while the sense of tragic impotence comes through the drooping inward swing of the arms. In the two preceding types, the arms are compressed into a single but energetic line. The form is horizontal rather than vertical and it is as if they were about to spring apart. In this last type, the tension is vertical and the inward swing of the arms makes them look as if they were pinioned, as if the figure with the erect frame and powerful head was helplessly weak. The absence of the weapon contributes to this attitude while the blank and staring eyes, the thin mouth, the flat impassive face and the slim vertical form evoke the calm resignation of the doomed.

In this last type, the will to a vital geometry reaches its height. The geometric rhythms convey an abstract exaltation, the beauty of a formal posture. At the same time they evoke a majestic super-human type. They convey the pathetic dignity of a sentenced hero, the tragedy of a vertical man.

[1] Plates 3, 7, 43 and 46; the phrase from a poem by Louis MacNeice.

Chapter Two

THE RITUAL OF THE CATTLE-GOD

I

THESE powerful and intriguing forms at once give rise to a number of problems. Why should the styles project these vital types? Why should they express this zest for vital geometry? To answer these questions, it is obvious that we must go to all the circumstances which surround their making. But before we ask why the styles are what they are, we must first inquire why they should exist at all. For in a peasant society, sculpture is never commissioned lightly. Its object is hardly ever simple decoration, the mere adornment of a harsh land. On the contrary its creation is normally impelled by vital needs. The two styles of West Bihar sculpture are both linked to a religious cult and if we are to explain their existence we must first examine their part in ritual.

II

We have already seen that the images are concerned with a cattle-god, Bir Kuar. The worship of this god centres on his primary function of actively aiding the Ahirs and of preserving them from harm. In the majority of Ahir villages his main task is to cause she-buffaloes to come on heat, and for this purpose bargains are made and special offerings are given. But besides this fertilizing function, Bir Kuar is also believed to exercise a general influence on the herds. Consequently, although his active help is only sought in accelerating pregnancies, sickness in a herd or attack by tiger are often thought to be due to his displeasure. And even in years when no special promise is to be redeemed, a certain minimum annual worship is done—partly as a caste habit but also from a feeling that it will insure against the effects of anger. In 1938, the Ahirs of Rohtas Kila delayed for some reason in doing the worship and they then began to notice that tigers were coming up to their houses. They therefore hurried up the

THE VERTICAL MAN

worship and after this the tigers went away. No actual harm had resulted, but there was a general feeling that the worship had been done none too soon.

The most general time at which the worship is performed is at the Sohrai Festival in October. Among the Kishnaut Ahirs this is pre-eminently the festival of Bir Kuar; but its observance is not confined to Kishnauts and throughout Bihar it is observed as a general cattle festival under the sponsorship of Krishna.

I

Who commanded the Dashara?
Who decreed the five days?
Who commanded Sohrai
And the dance of the cows?
Raja Dasrath commanded the Dashara
Ram decreed the five days
Krishna commanded Sohrai
And the dance of the cows.

2

Sohrai comes but once a year
And the girls worship Gaura and Ganesh
Going into the courtyards they light the lamps
And the flames go to the sky
Who observes the Dashara?
Who observes the five days?
Who worships at Sohrai?
Who worships on the sixth Sunday?
Dasrath observes Dashara
The gentry worship on the five days
Krishna observes Sohrai
And the mothers worship on the sixth Sunday.[1]

It is with the worship of Krishna that it probably originated,

---

[1] The five days are the five holy Sundays—the first Sunday of the bright halves of the Hindi months of Aghan, Pus, Magh, Phagun and Chait. These days are particularly holy. The sixth Sunday is the Sunday in the sixth month, Baisakh. Gaura is the wife of Shiva and Ganesh is their elephant son. The Dashara celebrates the victorious expedition of Ram to Lanka when he overcame Ravan and rescued Sita, Dasrath's daughter.

THE RITUAL OF THE CATTLE-GOD 27

and the Kishnaut Ahirs have specialized the festival by merging Krishna in Bir Kuar.

III

ORDINARY WORSHIP

The Festival lasts for sixteen days in Kartik (October) and culminates in the day following Diwali.

Six days before the Sohrai and again for six days after the festival has started, *dohas* or songs in praise of Bir Kuar are sung. These are not unlike Christmas carols which are sung for a week or ten days before Christmas and then on up to New Year's Eve. They range over all aspects of his character investing him sometimes with a naïve innocence, sometimes with majestic grandeur, at once celebrating his name and on occasion imploring him to regard the herds with favour.

3

Baba Bir Kuar, I offer you milk and *gur*
Protect me
Very small was Baba Birnath, brother
But he quickly killed a tiger.

4

O Bir Kuar baba, you are very bold
You wield two swords
One you keep under your arm
And with the other
You protect the world.

5

O Bir Kuar baba, blessed is your name
When I call upon you my cow conceives
And with her milk I feed you.

THE VERTICAL MAN

6

From that dense jungle
Where no sound issues
And no light enters
And where two tigers roar
Through the grace of Bir Kuar baba
The tigers go away
And the cows
Eat undisturbed.

7

The shrine of Baba Bir Kuar
Is west of the village
All the village worships him
Wherever our cows graze and wander
Protect them.

8

Brothers, my tawny cow is very good
Cow, you may wander where you will
Through the grace of Bir Kuar baba
I shall not need a stick.

9

O Bir Kuar baba
I remember your name always
And call upon it
Through your strength
I wander in the world
Protect me.

10

In a basket
Are rice and sandal wood
In a basket
Are flowers
O Bir Kuar baba
Come down
The annual day
Has come.

THE RITUAL OF THE CATTLE-GOD 29

11

Baba, of this place are you
But your name I do not know
I offer you milk and sugar
Protect me
On a black horse is Birnath
On a white horse is Bhagwan
Birnath comes on a stool of gold
To see his sons and grandsons.

12

Which is the birth place of Birnath, brother?
And where was he reared?
Where should his posts be put
And where is he honoured?
In Ayodhya was Birnath born
In Palamau he was reared
His posts are in the open fields
And there the people honour him.

13

Whose head
Has the red cloth?
Whose hair
Is matted with ashes?
Whose neck
Is graced with a garland?
Whose body
Shines with the rent silk?
The head of Birnath
Is decked in the red cloth
Chulhai Kuar
Is beautified with the matted hair
Langra Kuar
Is graced with a garland
Mother Jasoda
Shines with the rent silk.

THE VERTICAL MAN

14

Little is the image of Baba Birnath, brother
His thighs are a plantain post
His chest is a potter's wheel
His moustache is the head of a spear
His biceps are knotted wood
Under his armpit he holds a quiver
With nine hundred heads
And with a hook he kills his quarry.

15

What is the dais made of
And who has carved it?
Who sits on it?
Who cleans his mouth?
Whose thirty-two teeth are gleaming?
The dais is of wood
The carpenter has carved it
Baba Bir Kuar cleans his mouth
His thirty-two teeth are shining.

16

Red is the face of Birnath
And double are the barrels of his gun
Hunting in the jungle
He kills a tiger
But though he slays a tiger
He also shoots some partridges.[1]

[1] Just as the fifteenth-century wall painters in the Church of St. Peter and Paul, Pickering, Yorkshire, found it natural to paint Salome in the costume of a fifteenth-century glamour girl, Ahirs also assume that the world of Bir Kuar is no different from the world of today.

The following song from an early English morality play refers to Christ in very similar terms.

> Hail, darling dear, full of godhead
> I pray thee to be near when that I have need
> Hail: sweet is thy cheer; my heart would bleed
> To see thee sit here in such poor weed

THE RITUAL OF THE CATTLE-GOD 31

17

In the silent jungle grows a bamboo clump
Out of the bamboo is your shrine made, Birnath
Above and below it the royal geese play.

18

From the east comes a Turkinia[1]
And spins fine thread
With the thread is sewn a jacket
And Birnath wears it as he sits.

19

I spun and wove a cloth of gold
And on it my Baba reclines
Like an Emperor of Delhi.

For the same period of the festival some *ghi* is put on the posts or the images, usually each morning but occasionally in the evening. In many villages, the women quietly put the *ghi* on at night and only in villages where the cult is at a low ebb do the posts or images ever lack their *ghi*.

On the night of Diwali, that is, the night preceding Sohrai day, the Ahirs like other castes worship Lakshmi (or Bhagwati). Fortune marks consisting frequently of small black circles with white dots are painted on each side of their doors and rows of earthen lamps are placed on the verandahs. At the same time, a few earthen lamps[2] are placed before the shrine of Bir Kuar and left to burn themselves out, through the night.

The worship proper is done the following morning. The Ahirs

> With no pennies
> Hail: put forth thy dall
> I bring thee but a ball
> Have and play thee withal
> And go to the tennis.
>
> (A. W. Pollard, *English Miracle Plays, Moralities and Interludes* (Oxford, 1927), 42.)

[1] A female Jolaha or member of a Muhammadan weaving caste.
[2] See Plate 37.

THE VERTICAL MAN

assemble at the shrine, and a small fire is made. Some cows are then milked and after the milk has been boiled and some *gur* added, a preparation known as *khir* results. Some of this is then put on a leaf in front of the shrine. At the same time, some straw is put on a tile and *hum* is made by adding a little *ghi*. The straw is lit and the tile is placed so that the smoke from the *hum* goes up in front of the shrine. In addition to the *khir, thekua, gur, puris,* and *laung ka chhak*,[1] are sometimes offered. At the time of offering, Ahirs who feel like doing so bow before the shrine and after folding their hands offer a simple prayer in the following form. "Bir Kuar Baba, through your goodness my buffaloes have come on heat. Continue to protect them."

IV

THE MINOR FIGURES

But besides the offerings to Bir Kuar, subsidiary offerings are almost always made to one, two and sometimes three extra figures. These figures may be grouped into

1. personified elements of the main myth of Bir Kuar,
2. local accretions to the myth based on actual incidents or local needs, and
3. cult figures of other castes who are locally associated with Bir Kuar.

All three groups are influenced by the varying social atmospheres of the area and I give below a chart indicating the names under which the figures appear.

MINOR FIGURES

Relatives of Bir Kuar	Village
Children	
A son	Maharajganj
Brothers	
Langru Bir	Tendua
	Chandargarh

[1] See glossary.

9. URDANA

10. TENDUA, tola Ratanpura

11. DARANAGAR

12. BHISRA

13. TILOKHAR

14. NISHUNPUR

15. BAKNAUR

16. DANGWAR

THE RITUAL OF THE CATTLE-GOD

Relatives of Bir Kuar	*Village*
Bir	Mirsarae
A brother who was killed by a tiger	Mirsarae

Associates, friends and companions	
A Muhammadan	Bankheta
	Mathurapur
	Churesar
	Bishunpur
	Goradih
A lame carpenter	Madhkupia
An unknown Rajput	Dinadag
	Rambandh
A Bhuiya	Bahiar Khurd
A carpenter	Bahiar Khurd
	Dinadag
	Muhammadganj
	Bankheta
A man killed by a tiger (Baghaut)	Pipardih
An anonymous Pathan	Baskatia
An unknown stranger with Muhammadan affinities	Chakla Makritola
A strange Hindu whose caste is unknown	Tipa
A nameless friend of low caste	Lakhea
An unknown companion	Mirsarae
	Nishunpur
	Purnadih
	Urdana
	Pandaria

Langru Bir	
(*a*) An unknown associate	Khaira
	Sheikhpura
	Amba
	Ararua Kalan
	Khatin
	Kharwardih

C

Associates, friends and companions	Village
Langru Bir—*continued*	
(*a*) An unknown associate—*continued*	Tenudih tola of Sarma
	Banwari
	Chachayia
	Khajuri
	Barahi
(*b*) A Muhammadan	Ghunabigha
	Samauta
	Majhiyawan
	Benibigha
	Simarbari
	Arjundih
	Rambandh
(*c*) A lame carpenter	Tipa
(*d*) An Ahir	Narari
Gopi Mian, a Muhammadan	Khajuri
	Madhkupia
	Daranagar
	Turki
Tulsi Bir, a Bhuiya	Rudwa
Gop Gwal	Darahi
Madho Dank, a Bhuiya	Sitalpur
	Dumarchatti
Vishva Karma, a carpenter	Dhoba
Servants	
A cowherd	Chapra
	Tilauthu
	Maharajganj
A second cowherd	Maharajganj
An unknown servant	Selupara
A Jolaha servant	Nimahat
A *pahardār* (or body-guard)	Parha
	Tendua
	Rudwa
A *begar* (or "fag")	Indrapura
	Baradih
	Ananditchak
	Parcha

THE RITUAL OF THE CATTLE-GOD

Associates, friends and companions	*Village*
A favourite servant	Tumba
A Gorait (or drummer)	Nawadih
Langru Bir	
(*a*) an unknown servant	Chatra
(*b*) An Ahir servant	Khajuri
(*c*) a carpenter who was also a servant	Chatra
Gopi Mian	
(*a*) A Muhammadan cowherd	Khajuri
(*b*) A Jolaha servant	
Tulsi Bir, a body-guard	Mali
Bir	Jamuni
Goraiya, a Dusadh body-guard	Ramgarh
Seri, a body-guard	Basaura
Outsiders	
A Pathan servant of a landlord	Pipardih
	Tardih
	Uchaila
	Milki
	Babhantalao tola of Rohtas
	Kanker
A Khan Sahib	Daranagar
A Muhammadan dealer in bangles	Ramna
Sheikh Babal, a Muhammadan servant of the carpenter	Muhammadganj
Gopi Mian, a Pathan servant of a landlord	Jaintipur
Langru Bir, a Pathan servant of a landlord	Kanker
Pets	
A dog	Madhurampur

When offerings have been made to one or more of these extra figures, the remaining *khir* is distributed among the Ahirs present and the group disperses.

On such occasions of routine worship a medium is not usually called in and the worship becomes almost entirely a group act.

36 THE VERTICAL MAN

A particular Ahir acts as a leader but all the Ahirs see what is needed and while some prepare the *khir* and *thekua*, others make the *hum*. The worship is almost an exact instance of the operation of Rousseau's "general will."

V

THE EXPANDED WORSHIP

This routine worship is greatly expanded in years when a goat is sacrificed and in many villages a medium is summoned in order to lead it. On these occasions, the roots of the ceremony usually go back to many months prior to the actual Sohrai day, and the rites are simply the culmination of a process which includes

> a *bakauthi* or bargain with Bir Kuar
> the answer to the prayer
> the purchase of a goat in redemption of the promise
> the summoning of a medium
> the boiling of the village milk
> the goat sacrifice
> the offerings
> the medium's ecstasy
> the pantomime of the tiger
> and finally, the drama of the lame man.

The *bakauthi*.—The bargain which starts the process of expanded worship is usually made by a villager when there is abnormal delay in a she-buffalo coming on heat. The period of a buffalo's pregnancy is ten months and buffaloes are covered from the age of five years onwards. A she-buffalo usually calves between three to eight times, and the maximum normal "wait" between becoming pregnant and again coming into heat is three years. The months in which she-buffaloes usually come on heat are Asar and Sawan (June to August). If therefore a buffalo has not come into heat within two years of calving and the next Asar passes, the owner is filled with anxiety and if the delay goes on, he makes a solemn promise or bargain with Bir Kuar to sacrifice a goat or even to erect images in return for the weakness being remedied.

This is almost invariably the only matter for which bargains

THE RITUAL OF THE CATTLE-GOD 37

are made with Bir Kuar—the bringing of buffaloes into heat; and this is by far his major function. But just as throughout the area there are villages where his powers seem slightly more general, one also finds occasional villages where bargains are made to cover illness in the family or failure of crops, and in one village, Koeridih, a bargain had even been made for obtaining a child. In 1932, a childless Ahir of this village agreed to put up two stone images if he got a child. A little later his wife conceived and when the child was born two images were installed. But desolation succeeded delight for some time afterwards the child died. This is the only instance I know in which Bir Kuar was moved for increasing human fertility. It is for fertilizing she-buffaloes that nineteen out of twenty bargains are made.

The answer to the prayer.—Bir Kuar is first and foremost a "utility" god, and whether an Ahir fulfils a promise depends entirely on whether Bir Kuar has first fulfilled his part.

The promise is usually made at the shrine at night and in private and the existence of the bargain may thus be either public knowledge or a private secret. But the Ahir who makes it, knows that whether the village hears of it or not, Bir Kuar has heard and once his object has been achieved, he knows that he cannot lightly postpone completing the bargain. I give four instances in which posts and images formed the basis of the bargain. As the expenditure was greater than that involved in a goat, there was a greater element of hesitation but otherwise they are typical of all these bargains.

In Ramdihra, one of Deni Ahir's she-buffaloes had failed to come on heat. The delay became serious and he then promised Bir Kuar that if she again became fertile and gave him another she-buffalo, he would put up an image. The buffalo soon after came on heat and he got first one and then a second she-buffalo from her. He did not, however, keep the promise and, in fact, made no attempt to do so. Six of his she-buffaloes then suddenly died from cow-pox. Not long after, Bir Kuar appeared in a dream and told him that his herd would again increase only if he redeemed the promise. He then hurriedly commissioned the image and since then the herd has been recovering.

In Uchaila, Ram Nandan Pathak, a Brahman, had difficulty with his she-buffaloes and promised a stone image if they came

38 THE VERTICAL MAN

on heat. They did so and in 1935 he redeemed the promise and brought an image from Ramdihra.

In the Turki tola of Daranagar, Somaru Ahir put up two stone images in 1936. Here also there was some delay in implementing the promise and it was only after Bir Kuar had appeared in a dream and threatened to punish him, that he took steps to complete the bargain.

Finally, in Mahesara, an Ahir made a bargain that if the herd increased from five to fifty he would put up two posts. He died some years ago but when the herd did in fact reach fifty, his son honoured the bargain and in 1933 the posts were installed.

We may say then that the normal Ahir attitude is not to pay until the object has been accomplished but once it has been achieved, to make no bones about honouring the pledge.

The purchase of a goat.—For the purpose of sacrifice, a goat must not have been picked by a crow, bitten by a dog, or have ever been stolen. It must also be three years old and of only one colour. If a goat of these qualifications is available, it is bought about a month before the ritual date and is then duly offered. But if one is not forthcoming an ordinary goat is bought and the ceremony has to be delayed for three years while it roams freely. I was told that such cases are not common, and in any case, many villages are not very strict. But the theory exists and where the Ahirs are strongly religious, it is normally followed.

The extent to which goats are sacrificed varies very greatly. In some villages, a single goat is always sacrificed whether there is a promise to be redeemed or not. In others, years may elapse before a bargain becomes necessary, while in villages where belief in bargains is strong, the number of goats sacrificed in a year may be as many as three. In the Turki tola of Daranagar, two goats were sacrificed in 1937 and three in 1938. The latter included one from a Brahman and one from a Nunia.

The summoning of the medium.—When the goat has been arranged, the next step is to summon the *chhatia* or medium. There is usually a medium within a radius of five miles and on such occasions, information is sent to him and he comes over to preside at the rites.

A medium is qualified for his part less by any rites or knowledge than by the declaration that Bir Kuar comes regularly on

THE RITUAL OF THE CATTLE-GOD

him. It is the power to *khel*—to go through a paroxysm and achieve a climax—that is his main qualification. He is, as it were, the sensitiser who picks up the god, the body which temporarily receives him. He goes through a form of hysterical exaltation during which the god absorbs him and he in turn absorbs the god. When it is over, he sinks back in an ecstasy of relief.

The boiling of the milk.—The ritual day then comes. When the medium has arrived, the Ahirs move over to the shrine. Incense is prepared. The medium puts on a new *dhoti*. All the village milk is collected and a trench, five to ten feet long, is dug. In this, a fire of wood is lit. A big earthen pot full of the milk is then put on it, a little rice is added and the milk is boiled up until a skin forms. The medium then squats on the pot and tosses the skin over his shoulders, sprinkling it at random. In Deuria and Tenua Dusadhi, the milk is put into seven pots on the trench and when the milk is boiling the medium walks on the pots five or six times and as he walks he scoops up the skin and tosses it in the air.

In most villages the walking on the pots coincides with the start of the ecstasy, but in Bahiar Khurd it occurs when the medium is well into the frenzy and is in fact used to test whether or not Bir Kuar is actually on him. In this village, the medium comes out of the jungle moving on all fours like a tiger and nosing hither and thither. The Ahirs call on him to dip his hand into the boiling milk and sprinkle the skin. If he does this without being scalded, it is plain that Bir Kuar has possessed him. The medium pays no immediate heed to the challenge and goes nosing round and round. Then when he feels the moment has come, he hunches himself up on the pot, darts his fingers into the milk and throws the skin over his shoulders with a slick and easy gesture.

The goat sacrifice.—With the sprinkling of the skin the stage for sacrificing the goat is reached.

But before this can take place, the goat must first be tested. This sometimes takes the form of putting flowers and vermilion on its head and if the head shakes, Bir Kuar is believed to have accepted it. Or instead of putting flowers on the head, the horns are rubbed with vermilion and a little rice is put on the ground before it. If the goat eats the rice, it is again considered

THE VERTICAL MAN

that Bir Kuar has assented. If the goat's head does not shake or the rice is not eaten, the goat is released and re-offered in a year's time. If, after one year, it still does not make the proper response, it is released and re-offered once a year until it signifies assent.

If the test is satisfactory, the head is then struck off and lifted up and placed on the shrine. The liver is extracted, cooked and put on the shrine and some liquor is poured over it. The carcase is then cut up and distributed; and to prevent the crows picking them, the bones are buried at the spot. In villages such as Bagen, the custom is to cook the meat away from the spot (though never outside the village) while in villages such as Ganguli, the flesh is cooked then and there. In the Babhantalao tola of Rohtas, the liver is made into a ball, cooked, split up into five parts and then offered.

The actual ritual for severing the head varies widely from region to region. The normal method is to use either a sacrificial sword, a *balua* or a *hansua*. The sword resembles a heavy butcher's chopper and a single weighted stroke is sufficient for neatly severing the neck. The same applies to a *balua* which is a kind of halberd, with the head fitted to a stout stick. The *balua* is gripped in both the hands and a slick cut is made with it. The *hansua* is a large sickle with a keen cutting edge with which the neck is sawn off. It is usual for the Ahir offering the goat to execute it.

In contrast to these forms each of which is strictly practical, there is a form with ritual significance. This is the beheading with a *bansula* or a carpenter's adze. When it is used the goat is held down with its neck on a block of wood and its head is then hacked off in four or five strokes. The first drops of blood are put on the *bansula* as an act of worship to the carpenter. The blood from the neck is then collected, mixed with milk and drunk by the medium. In Madhkupia this rite is accompanied by a separate offering to a lame carpenter and wherever possible, as in Rambandh, Muhammadganj and other villages of Hussainabad, a carpenter is brought in to do the execution. In Sonbarsa there is the added requirement that the carpenter who does the beheading must belong to the same family as that of the carpenter who made the posts. To the meaning of this rite I shall return later.

THE RITUAL OF THE CATTLE-GOD 41

When the killing is over, there is usually nothing to commemorate it. But a marked exception is in the Aurangabad area where the sacrifice is always accompanied by the insertion of two pegs in the ground. These pegs are made of *bel* wood and are put in only when a goat is sacrificed and only when the goat is offered by an Ahir. The pegs are provided each year, free of charge, by the local carpenter, but as they are small, they rarely remain in place for more than a few weeks. In Itkhori *thana*, there is a similar usage. In Nagwa and Dhankheri, a post is put up whenever a goat is sacrificed, and in this way each village has acquired thirty to forty posts. In the Bahera tola of Gondaria there are as many as forty-five posts. As the posts are much taller than the pegs used in Aurangabad, the posts have remained where they were installed. Elsewhere, a discoloured patch near the shrine is all that marks the killing.

The medium's ecstasy.—After the goat has been sacrificed, the medium starts his frenzy. He puts on a new saffron-coloured *dhoti*, approaches the shrine and prepares incense. His body then starts to quiver, his arms shake and he is tossed from spot to spot. In the course of the frenzy, he catches hold of the images, mounts them, or leaning heavily, goes round and round. If there are clay horses, he puts his toes on them, "rides" them for a few moments and then climbs the posts. In various villages in Chatarpur *thana*, he carries a hair cord with which he strikes himself and the Ahirs.[1] This ecstatic ambulation then merges into the two final episodes—the pantomimes of the tiger and the lame man.

The pantomime of the tiger.—This performance occurs in villages where the cult of "the man killed by the tiger" (Baghaut) is strong and where additional offerings are made to him during the worship of Bir Kuar. It sometimes follows, but more usually precedes, the pantomime of the lame man, and the two dramas then blend in one. In a village such as Mananpur, the two are telescoped and the lame man turns into the tiger on his way to the shrine.

The first pantomime goes as follows. In Lawadag, when the offerings are over, the goat's head is taken four yards to the front and the medium ties his hair cord round the horns or ears.

[1] Probably as a purification from evil spirits.

42 THE VERTICAL MAN

He then simulates a tiger and slinks about on all fours, finally pouncing on the head, putting an ear between his teeth, worrying it and, at last, tossing it away with a jerk of the head. In the Tendua tola of Ratanpura the goat's head is hidden by one of the Ahirs and the medium then pretends to be a tiger and slinks about, looking for it. When he finds it, he sniffs it and returns. In Basantbigha also, the goat's head is hidden and the medium ramps and roars like a tiger, creeping round on all fours and glaring till he finds it. He then takes an ear in his teeth and shakes it.

The pantomime of the lame man.—The medium now changes to a lame man. There is not, however, any standard pattern to which this drama must conform and it varies widely from village to village. Thus, in Lawadag, two of the Ahirs present are nominated as *begars* (men who are compelled to do cooliework without any pay). They are given a few *puris* but after eating them they ask for more. A mock negotiation follows. At last, the amount of their food is settled and some cloth is made up into a bundle. One of the *begars* takes up the bundle and puts a hand under the medium's armpit while the other *begar* supports him on the other side. The medium carries two sticks and assisted by the *begars*, he hobbles a distance of ten yards. The *begars* then suddenly push him down and run away. The medium picks himself up and this ends the paroxysm.

In Sunri the pantomime is slightly different. As soon as the offerings are over, a *begar* is chosen, some *puris* are put in a bundle on his head, and he is told to go in front. The medium has two sticks—one a short one and one a long one. He limps after the *begar* with his foot resting half way up the long stick. He then throws the short stick at the *begar* who drops the bundle, breaks the long stick in two, and falls down. Finally, he picks himself up and walks to the posts. The stick which he has thrown at the *begar* is now brought back to him, he anoints it with milk and *gur* and gives it back to the owner. In Ramgarh, on the other hand, wraps are put on the shoulders of two men and the medium puts his arms round their necks and supports himself. They then advance six to ten paces when the *begars* push the medium over and run away. The medium rolls himself back to the posts where he bows and pours water on the ground. In

THE RITUAL OF THE CATTLE-GOD   43

Muhammadganj the medium pretends to be lame and hunches
up a leg. A man then pretends to be a coolie and is given some
roti, which he puts on his head. He then sets off as if carrying
a load and as he passes the medium, the latter tells him to
stop and tries to snatch the *roti*. The man does not pay any
attention. The medium threatens him and finally he throws
a stick after him. On this, the coolie takes to his heels, the
medium limps after the stick, recovers it and returns to the
shrine where he bows his head. In Barka Tiaria there is a curious
deviation. At the end of the offerings the medium stoops down
and moves about six yards from the shrine in a hunched-up
manner holding a *chhar*, the rope used for tying the legs of
buffaloes. He imitates the posture of a lame man but does not
carry a stick and there is no interlude with a *begar* or a bundle.
Similarly in Khajuri the element of the mock assault is lacking
and there is instead a strange meeting between Bir Kuar and the
lame brother, Langru Bir. At the close of the offerings, a man
(not the medium) leans on a stick, pretends to be lame and acts
the part of Langru Bir. The medium, who pretends to be Bir
Kuar, climbs on his back and is carried a few steps until the lame
man stumbles and collapses. Other men help the lame man to
his feet—while the medium bows down where he fell. Finally,
in Mananpur there is a curious fusion with the tiger pantomime.
A man is selected and fed with *puris* and is then given a bundle.
He supports the medium and they advance ten yards. He then
pushes the medium down and throws away the bundle. The
medium then picks up the bundle in his teeth and crawls back
to the post—his return signifying that Bir Kuar has left him.

The pantomime of the horse.—In Kurasin, I came across a casual
recollection of a third pantomime. An old Ahir said that when
he was a boy, he saw the pantomime of the horse. The medium
selected a man, made him pretend to be a horse and sent him
racing off for a distance of two hundred yards. There was no
mimicry of galloping. He then called him back with a shout
and the horse left the man as he reached the shrine.

Termination.—With the ending of the pantomime the celebra-
tions end and the Ahirs disperse.

THE VERTICAL MAN

VI

THE CLAY HORSES

In many villages in Rohtas thana and the Sadr subdivision of Palamau, little clay horses are offered[1]—sometimes as supplements to goats and sometimes as substitutes for them. They are usually fired and are a sunny red colour, but occasionally, the clay is left soft and they then remain a dirty yellow. Like the carpenters who supply the posts, the potters who model them do so as a duty and not for sale, receiving in return either a pice or a *pawa* of gram.

When the horse is the main offering, it occupies the place in the worship which is otherwise taken by the goat. On other occasions when it is only subsidiary, it is offered along with *khir*, *thekua, puris* and sweets. Its object is to provide Bir Kuar with a steed, a form of celestial conveyance and so to win his favour.

> "Let not the reckless heavenly riders
> Treat him or me as rank outsiders."[2]

VII

THE INSTALLATION OF POSTS AND IMAGES

While the offer of a goat is the commonest form of bargain the installation of wooden posts or stone images is the extreme kind and it is here that we approach the function of the sculpture. The offer of images is made at times of major crisis. It is a form of bargain which will secure favour when nothing else will. In years when images are erected, goats are also sacrificed and the worship follows the normal expanded type with the addition of the installation ceremony.

The installation of the images.—These ceremonies are essentially fluid and vary with the means of the Ahir.

In Bank, when an image is put up, the custom is for the carpenter to bring the figure to the site, and after ceremonially receiving a present, to place it in the hands of the Ahir who is

[1] See Plates 23, 29, 33, 34, 37, 38 and 45. [2] W. H. Auden.

THE RITUAL OF THE CATTLE-GOD 45

dedicating it. The Ahir then sprinkles it with water, washes it with turmeric, anoints it with *achhat* and sandal wood and then plants it in the ground. A *dhoti* or a wrap is put round the post. The Ahir then makes a circle of the cattle present and offers a prayer to Bir Kuar.

In Kundari, two wooden figures were put up in 1935. The posts were brought by the carpenter, washed in water and rubbed with turmeric. Two holes were then dug and a pie and a betel nut placed in each. The posts were put in and a *dhoti* was wrapped round them. A Brahman recited installation verses.

In Tilauthu, two stone images were erected in 1932. The mason was given a cow worth six rupees, a *dhoti* and one rupee in cash. The images were brought to the spot on the morning of Sohrai, washed with water and anointed with *haldi* and *ghi*. Then they were set up in position, incense was made and they were again smeared with *ghi*. Finally a goat was sacrificed and *tapawan* prepared.

VIII

THE DANCE OF THE COWS

At the end of the sacrifice or installation, the Ahirs unite in a general celebration of the cattle, "a dance of the cows." This is the climax of the Sohrai, the gala with which the *puja* ends, the mass rite which clinches the worship and ushers the Ahirs into another year.

The Bhojpuri term for this rite is *gaidarh*. *Gai* means cow or cows while *darh* is a term used only in connection with the rite. If one asks an Ahir what *darh* means, he always replies *gai darh*. The term is sometimes expanded into *gai nachne ka darh*—the *darh* of the dancing cows. The "dance of the cows" seems, therefore, the nearest English equivalent, for it retains the sound of the original and hints also at the solemn lumbering dance in which the spectacle consists.

The ritual has possibly two meanings. Dr. J. H. Hutton states that "the doctrine of soul-substance as a fertiliser is not less applicable to animals than to human beings, and it is therefore not surprising to find the Malas of Southern India and Ahirs at

THE VERTICAL MAN

the Gaidaur festival causing their cattle—the young in particular—to trample a pig to death, after which, according to ancient custom, the corpse of the pig is eaten."[1]

Another view is that the pig is a scapegoat, an animal on to which the weaknesses and blemishes of the herd are transferred; and this possibly receives confirmation from the fact that in certain villages, a calf is used as proxy for the pig and the slaughter is replaced by a chase.

The dance itself is performed as follows. The cows and buffaloes are rounded up and after they have been sanctified with *ghi* and vermilion, a pig is swung into their midst on a rope. The animals come towards it, butt it with their horns and then prance over it. As the dance goes on, the animals get wilder and the pig is tossed high in the air. Finally, an animal gores or tramples on it and with its death the dance ends.

During my tour in 1938, I saw two dances—one at Ghunabigha and the other at Naykagaon in Rohtas *thana*.

At Ghunabigha, it was already late in the afternoon and the sun was descending on the Rohtas hills. The preliminaries had been completed and the cattle were being driven in. A small sow had been placed in a hollow in a mango grove and thirty yards away the images of Bir Kuar looked grimly on.

There was a grassy open space all round the mango grove and cattle were arriving from three directions. The cows were herded separately from the buffaloes. Ahirs stood about with sticks and some had drums.

When the cattle had come in, three Ahirs went round them giving each some coarse country salt from a little basket and smearing some *ghi* on their horns from a leaf packet.

An old woman then came and put vermilion first on the drums then on the foreheads of the cows and finally on the horns of the buffaloes. After the vermilion had been put, a man went round the three herds and sprinkled a little liquor on the horns.

The drum then began to beat and the sow was got ready. A man stooped down beside it and tied a piece of rope about five yards long to the right back leg. A *lota* of water was brought and the water sprinkled on the sow. After that, the old woman sprinkled some vermilion on its forehead. Some rice was dropped

[1] J. H. Hutton, *Census of India*, 1931, *India*, I, 405.

THE RITUAL OF THE CATTLE-GOD 47

on its mouth, and the sow gobbled it up. The man with the bottle of liquor poured out a handful and sprinkled it on its mouth, and about the same time a cup full of liquor was poured on the ground in front of the Bir Kuar shrine.

The dance then started. Three Ahirs advanced towards the cows—one of them leading the sow, another singing and the third beating a drum. The sow was pitched into the herd, and after dilly-dallying a little a cow ran at it and butted it with its forehead. The Ahirs then drove the cows round and as each cow came up, it drove its head against the victim and then jumped over it. When the cows had finished the sow was led over to the buffaloes. In order to excite them, some of their calves were taken and dangled near it. This made the buffaloes frantic and they ran at the sow. Occasionally the rope got hitched to the horns of a buffalo and the sow was swung about.

I watched the process for half an hour and there then appeared little likelihood of the animal being killed. It had been bruised by the butting and it tried to lie as quietly as possible, but when the drummer struck it playfully four times, it came smartly to its feet and trotted off.

I then went on to Naykagaon where a similar dance was pending. Here the pig was put into the cattle almost at once, and as the cows were more savage, several attacked it together, butting and trampling on it. In less than five minutes, its limp and lifeless body was being swung among the horns, and when it rested on a furrow, the cows came and smelt its blood.

Elsewhere in the area dances follow the same type but here and there, a village develops its own variant. Thus in Hardaspur a mock pig is used. A *bhatua*, or vegetable like a marrow, is wrapped up in a torn blanket, made into a bundle and dragged about among the cattle. The cattle are made to gore it with their horns and leap over it. Similarly in Uchaili a pig is not dragged but a rope is tied to a calf which is pulled through the herd. Other villages have other local expressions.

With the termination of the rite, the Ahirs go home and the day ends with the worship of their household dead and with stick-dancing and drinking.

THE VERTICAL MAN

IX

CONCLUSION

In this long and intricate ritual, the role of the sculpture is clear. It marks the shrine of Bir Kuar and focusses Ahir attention on the ritual. It advertises the potent function of the god. But above all it is an offering to Bir Kuar, a means of purchasing his favour, a way of honouring him. It is put up in return for she-buffaloes coming on heat and is promised because its installation is thought to please Bir Kuar and satisfy his needs. It is because Bir Kuar demands the images and in return for receiving them will make the buffaloes fertile that the styles of sculpture exist.

17. TENUA DUSADHI

18. SHEIKHPURA

19. SHANKARPUR

20. BARADIH

21. BASANT BIGHA

22. MANHANIA

23. AMAHUA

24 CHURESAR

Chapter Three

THE MYTH OF BIR KUAR

I

INTRODUCTION

IF the immediate cause of the sculpture, the reason for its existence, is the Ahir need of bringing buffaloes on heat, we have still to see why the Ahirs should credit Bir Kuar with a need for sculpture, and why in satisfaction of it the figures should assume their strange and powerful shapes. To resolve these questions we must go to the story of Bir Kuar itself and I will now describe the myth which dominates the ritual and gives the cult its vital power.

The life and death of Bir Kuar is recounted in several full narratives and is sometimes celebrated in *chānchars* or long sagas which are sung by the Ahirs at night. Not all Ahirs, however, recall these songs and the myth is sometimes only a sentence briefly describing Bir Kuar's function. These meagre phrases are obviously of much less value than the longer versions yet we must not ignore their contents. Once a myth has decayed, the summary which passes for it may be due to two causes. Either it is a genuine fragment of the main myth—surviving while the rest has been eaten away or it is a local substitute developed to explain the worship or the shrine. In the latter case, a complex of local influences may cause it to sprout in unexpectedly distorting forms. Yet equally with the major narratives, these forms are clues to Ahir needs. They supplement the main accounts. They state what Ahirs believe and expect from Bir Kuar and it is through the sum of all these versions that the myth reveals the nature of the god.

II

SUMMARY OR SUBSTITUTE LEGENDS

In the greater part of the area, the legend is merely the name and no attempt is made to go beyond this final blank. The name

THE VERTICAL MAN

is connected with the shrine and the function, and after this, there is no knowledge either of the caste, the family or the death.

In another rudimentary form, the legend is the casteman. In Bahera, for instance, an Ahir said "Bir Kuar was an Ahir and we do not know if he is dead." In Shankarpur another Ahir told me "Bir Kuar was an Ahir. He died but we do not know why." In this simple form—merely linking the god to the caste—the legend continues in villages such as Turki, Tiara Kurd and Longraha.

In the next stage, Bir Kuar becomes both his wife and himself; and the legend is simply that he died and after his death his wife committed *sati*. This form is found particularly in Dehri and Rohtas *thānās* where the cult of Sati Devi is strong and where almost all the villages contain little double-breasted stones to mark a woman who has died in this manner. In this region, the two posts or the twin stones are regarded as male and female and the shrine explains the legend.[1]

A slight advance is made when the legend focusses on the function. In Dehri and Rohtas thanas, for instance, a common formula for describing Bir Kuar is that he was an Ahir who offered his life in the defence of cows—*gai ke gohar me jujh gaya*, and continues to protect them if he is worshipped.

This formula is slightly amplified in the next stage where the legend is not simply the function but also the method of death. In a curious form of which I found only one instance[2] the method of death implies the service of the cows. "Bir Kuar was an Ahir who along with two cowherds was trampled in a *gai dārh*. He had a wife and a son." They were killed, that is, while assisting the cattle in their annual rite. More usually, however, the death occurs as part of a definite effort to protect the cattle and in such cases Bir Kuar dies by combat.

"Bir Kuar and a cowherd were killed by a man while rescuing cattle which the man was taking away." (*Chapra*)

[1] In the sculpture the female figures, barring the primary sexual characters, are exact counterparts of the male.

[2] Maharajganj.

THE MYTH OF BIR KUAR

"Bir Kuar fought with a cattle thief and was killed. He appeared in a dream and said he would protect the cattle. His wife committed *sati*." (*Baradih*)

Three other examples spring from the same locality—an area where Mughal influence was strong and decaying mosques and graveyards still mark the land. They illustrate the kind of distortion to which a substitute legend is susceptible.

"Bir Kuar was killed in a fight while resisting the seizure of cattle by a Muhammadan ruler." (*Manharia*)

"Bir Kuar was killed in a fight with some Muhammadan butchers while attempting to rescue some cattle. His wife died on realizing he was dead." (*Ranjitganj*)

"During the Muhammadan period, the Muhammadans were impounding cattle and taking *ghi* and milk from the Ahirs by force. Bir Kuar, a brother named Bir and a third friend made a stand against it and were all killed while resisting the seizure of cows." (*Mirsarae*)

Finally, a stage is reached where although the legend is rudimentary, it ceases to be a substitute. It is not simply a local invention to explain the shrine. It contains a hint of the main myth. The forms taken at this stage are two. In the first, a tiger is introduced as the death-agent.

"Bir Kuar was an Ahir who was killed by a tiger while rescuing cattle." (*Katar*)

"Bir Kuar was killed by a tiger while grazing his buffaloes. He appeared in a dream and told his family to put up posts." (*Tilokhar*)

"Bir Kuar was an Ahir who was killed by a tiger while grazing his buffaloes. His buffalo, Paraiwa, took him to the tethering ground where he told his castemen to worship him." (*Gauhara*)

THE VERTICAL MAN

In the second, a witch is the death-agent.

"Bir Kuar was an Ahir who was killed by a witch."

(*Katar*)

"Bir Kuar met a witch in the jungle who fatally injured him." (*Lakhea*)

With the appearance of the tiger and the witch the substitute legends finish and we are on the road to the heart of the myth.

III

THE MAIN MYTH

The main myth can be analysed into three groups. In the first is the complete story, while in the second and third are what we may call branch legends. Each of these is separate from the other but in the main myth they coalesce.

The three forms may be summarized as follows.

According to the first branch, Bir Kuar was an Ahir who goes into the jungle to graze his buffaloes and comes on his sister practising witchcraft. With her are seven companions and all have taken off their clothes. He at first takes away the clothes but later he gives them back. Then the witches fearing scandal decide to get him killed. They send a tiger and Bir Kuar is fatally mauled. His pet buffalo carries him home and on his death bed he tells the Ahirs to worship him.

In the second branch, Bir Kuar quarrels with his sister and in consequence she gives a curse that a tiger will kill him. Bir Kuar does not pay any heed and goes into the jungle. When he enters it, a tiger mauls him. His pet buffalo then brings him home and he tells the Ahirs to worship him.

Thus, in the first form, it is the exposure of the witches which brings the tiger on Bir Kuar and causes his death; and in the second it is the curse of his sister which brings out the tiger and sends him to his doom.

These two accounts are caught up in the main myth and reconciled in the following ways—firstly, through the insistence (already present in the first form) that Bir Kuar's sister is herself a witch and secondly, through the first branch becoming the

THE MYTH OF BIR KUAR

means through which the second takes effect. Bir Kuar is cursed that if he goes into the jungle the tiger will get him. The tiger does get him, but only because through going into the jungle against the curse, he stumbles on the witches, and the witches set up the tiger.

On the basis of this structure the myth builds itself up. In no two villages is it quite the same, and, in fact, its vitality is gauged by the way it sprouts into new and vivid details. Through its flimsy and varying forms drift a number of fluid figures and their emphasis changes from village to village. These figures supplement the structure rather than conflict with it. Their effect is to charge the situation with added power and it is through their mysterious presence that the vital issues become clear.

IV

THE FIRST BRANCH LEGEND: THE WITCHES

The four legends which emphasize the witch motif spring from Tardih, Bahiar Khurd, Harihargunj and Chacharia.

Each is based on the same pattern, but each develops in a different way and stresses points which are of vital importance for the cult.

THE TARDIH LEGEND

According to this legend, "Bir Kuar was a Kishnaut Ahir. He had a sister, Kani Biramdeia who used to take seven girls into the jungle at night, and instruct them in witchcraft. For doing this, they used to strip themselves naked. One night Bir Kuar untied his buffaloes and was taking them through the jungle when he came on the spot where they were practising their art and saw them naked. He thought he would teach them a lesson, so he picked up their clothes and climbed a tree. When the witches came they found their clothes gone, and saw that some one was looking at them. They started to cry and Bir Kuar then returned their clothes. The girls dressed and started for the village. On the way they summoned a tiger which sprang on Bir Kuar and mauled his right leg. Bir Kuar cried out with pain and alarm and

54 THE VERTICAL MAN

his buffaloes, Parewa and Bhuwari, lifted him on their horns and began to move home. As they carried him, the blood from his leg trickled on their bells and clogged the sound. Bir Kuar's brother, Kuar, heard the muffled noise and wondering what had happened went to the western side of the village. There he met the two buffaloes bringing his brother. Bir Kuar told him he was dying and said that the Ahirs should put up a post to him to the west of the village and should worship him. Because of what she had done, his sister should not be given any dowry at her marriage."

In this form the fundamental points are:

Bir Kuar is killed because he acts as a moral man.

He does not show any great strength and is quite easily killed.

His visit to the jungle with his buffaloes is normal and natural. There is nothing out of the ordinary either in the time or in the act.

Two of his buffaloes show extreme devotion and his passage home on their backs is described with great clarity.

It is in his right leg that he is mauled and it is this which leads to his death.

The death-bed declaration results in his worship.

A brother—Kuar—appears, acts as the transmitter of his declaration and then disappears.

Bir Kuar's sister is named (Kani Biramdeia) but the act which kills Bir Kuar is an act of the witches as a group and is not specifically his sister's.

THE BAHIAR KHURD LEGEND

In the next form, Bir Kuar remains as the moral man who is destroyed by the forces of darkness but the emphasis shifts from his buffaloes to his own power as a fighter.

According to this legend, "Bir Kuar's sister was a witch. One night as he was going through the jungle he saw some lamps lit and his sister and six girls dancing naked around them. He went and took away their clothes. When they had finished dancing they went to put on their clothes but could not find them. They thought that only Bir Kuar could be wandering in the jungle at night and went after him. They reached him and asked him to give them back their clothes. He gave them back. The witches

THE MYTH OF BIR KUAR

then began to think that if Bir Kuar returned to the village he would tell what he had seen and that it would be safer to destroy him. Bir Kuar's sister said, 'He is my brother. How can I consent to have him killed?' The other witches said 'We will do it.' They began by sending a snake but Bir Kuar killed it. Then they sent Bir Kuar's sister in the form of a tigress and she pounced on Bir Kuar and mauled him. Bir Kuar's buffalo then picked him up and carried him home. When they got home, Bir Kuar's castemen came and Bir Kuar told them to put up posts to him and worship him and he would promote the welfare of their cattle. Then he died."

Here the following points are stressed:

Bir Kuar is killed only after the witches have tried once and failed. He exhibits strength but a tigress proves fatal.

There is a hint that Bir Kuar is entirely fearless, as he grazes his buffaloes in the jungle at night and is the only Ahir who does so.

His sister opposes his murder but not actively; and finally she becomes a passive instrument in the hands of her companions and turns into the tigress-agent which finally mauls him.

There is no brother but his castemen gather and receive his instructions.

THE HARIHARGANJ LEGEND

This magnification of Bir Kuar is continued and extended in the Hariharganj legend.

According to this legend, "Birnath was grazing his buffaloes in the jungle one *day* when he came on seven witches. They had stripped themselves naked and had put on short skirts made of brooms.[1] Birnath took their clothes over to where his buffaloes

---

[1] The association of brooms with witches is general in Europe and also in parts of India. Dehon, in describing witchcraft in the Mahuadanr area of Palamau district, states that "when a would-be Dain Bisahi (or witch) wishes to learn, she strips off her clothes and puts them near her *akhāra* or dancing place. She then puts on a peridzoma made with broken sticks of an old broom and goes to a cave which is a resort of Dains." (*The Religion and Customs of the Uraons*, 144.)

Verrier Elwin, in a private communication, considers that the broom may be a penis-substitute and notes that at Gond, Pardhan and Muria weddings in Mandla and Bastar a man sometimes fastens a broom to his crutch and waggles it like a large penis.

THE VERTICAL MAN

were grazing. When the witches had finished they were surprised to find their clothes gone and by a process of magic divined that Birnath had taken them. They decided to go to him each pretending to be one of his relatives—one his sister, one his mother, one his grandmother, and so on. When Birnath saw them he relented and gave the clothes back. The witches dressed and then began to think that if Birnath went back to the village he would spread the news of his discovery. So they decided to get him killed. First they sent a tiger but Birnath caught it, put a string through its nose, and rode it through the jungle.[1] Then the witches sent a tigress. When the tigress came, Birnath left the tiger. As he fought the tigress, the tiger attacked him. In this way Birnath kept fighting, first one and then the other. After a long struggle he grew exhausted and called to his buffalo, Parai, for help. Parai came and stood over him and fought them in turn with her horns. But she also grew exhausted and then the tiger and tigress sprang on Birnath and killed him. Parai put Birnath on her back and carried him to the tethering ground. Birnath then came on his brother, Chulhai Kuar, told him how he had died, and said that his castemen should worship him in return for his protecting their cattle."

In this legend there is no question of Birnath's strength, for he demonstrates his super-normal power by not only conquering the tiger but humiliating it. But the tigress remains fatal.

None of the witches is Birnath's sister but the sister motif is not entirely absent for it is in the guise of sister, mother and grandmother that the witches get their clothes back.

Birnath's special relation with his buffalo, Parai, is beginning to assume importance. She is not simply the chosen buffalo who carries him home but she is also the buffalo who fights for and protects him.

A new turn is given to the cult since it is neither in a dream nor on a death bed that Birnath makes his divine appeal. He comes

[1] In the Central Provinces, "a person who has ridden on a tiger brings luck. Consequently the Gonds and Baigas, if they capture a young tiger and tame it, will take it round the country, and the cultivators pay them a little to give their children a ride on it." (R. V. Russell and Hiralal, *The Tribes and Castes of the Central Provinces of India* (London, 1916), IV, 85.)

THE MYTH OF BIR KUAR

on his brother and the revelation is made while the brother is possessed.

THE CHACHARIA LEGEND

If these legends define the first "branch," it is with the version from Chacharia that the myth begins to move into its second form. The witch motif is still fundamental but it is Bir Kuar's relation with Paraiya, his buffalo, which now swamps the story. It is this situation which forms a major element in the second branch.

According to this version, "Bir Kuar had seven sisters all of whom were witches. On the night, at the hour before daybreak, when Bir Kuar had brought his wife for their *gaunā* or second marriage he went at the usual time for untieing his buffaloes and taking them into the jungle. In the jungle he came on the seven sisters stripped naked and engaged in magic. He picked up their clothes and took them away. When the sisters had finished, they began to look for their clothes, and when they heard the bell of Paraiya they concluded that only Birnath could have taken them. They then went to him and asked him to return their clothes. He refused. They then conferred and decided to send a snake to bite him. Paraiya sensed that some danger might come to Birnath and told him that he must not get separated from her but must sit on her back. Birnath climbed on her back and a little later a snake came, tried to swarm up Paraiya and reach him, but as the snake rose, Paraiya butted it with her horns and brushed it back with her legs. And presently the snake went away. The sisters then sent a scorpion thinking that it could get up without being seen and bring Birnath down by stinging him. The snake would then bite him. But Paraiya detected the scorpion and drove it away. The sisters then sent a tiger. Birnath felt thirsty and wanted water. Paraiya said she would take him to a stream where she would lower her head and he could drink while still remaining on her back. She told him he must not get down as otherwise he would be in danger. Birnath said, 'How can I drink from your neck?' Paraiya said, 'You must drink that way or not at all.' They reached the stream and went into the water. But Birnath could not reach the water from her head and came down

58 THE VERTICAL MAN

from her back.While he was drinking with his hands, the tiger came to the water and pounced upon him. After mauling him the the tiger went away. Paraiya then came, dipped her horns in Birnath's blood and galloped to his home, to show that something was wrong. Birnath's mother saw Paraiya coming before the usual time and when she saw the blood on her horns, she knew that Birnath was hurt. She and Birnath's wife and two or four neighbours then went with Paraiya to where Birnath was lying and there they found him on the point of death. Before he died, he told them to put up twin posts to him and worship him and he would safeguard their cattle."

Here the salient points are:

Birnath is in no sense a super-man. It is his buffalo who staves off the snake and the scorpion, and when he neglects her advice, the tiger has no difficulty in killing him.

The sister motif is given great importance. All the seven witches are Birnath's sisters and it is because of their hostility that Birnath dies.

Birnath does not show great devotion to his buffalo, but the buffalo exhibits the greatest love for Birnath.[1]

---

[1] For a parallel to Parai, compare Sigurd's charger, Grani, in the Norse poem, "The Old Lay of Gudrun."

> From the Thing came Grani—with thundering hoofs
> but lo! Sigurd—himself came not.
> The saddle-steeds all—with sweat were steaming
> long had they sped—the slayers bearing.

> Weeping I went—with Grani to whisper
> With tear-wet cheek—the charger questioned;
> Grani his head—in grief drooped,
> he knew that his master—lived no more.
>
> <div align="right">(Bertha S. Phillpotts, <i>Edda and Saga</i>, 58)</div>

"Grimm in his *Teutonic Mythology* remarks: 'One principal mark to know heroes by is their possessing intelligent horses, and conversing with them. The touching conversation of Achilles with his Xanthos and Balios finds a complete parallel in the beautiful Karling legend of Bayard.'" (N. M. Penzer, *The Ocean of Story* (London 1924–28), II, 57.)

Sir George Grierson has also drawn attention to a similar role of horses in the Rajput Lay of Alha. "Each of the heroes, he says, possesses a horse of fairy breed that saves him in many a difficult situation. For instance, Malkhan's mare, Kabutri, or 'the Pigeon,' is ridden by her master in a furious battle charge.

THE MYTH OF BIR KUAR

SUMMARY: THE FIRST BRANCH

We may now summarize the stages reached in the first "branch." Firstly, Bir Kuar is throughout treated as a moral man but not invariably as a strong man. The legend fluctuates between the view of him as a man easily killed by the tiger and the view that only after a long combat does the tigress kill him. In the Bahiar Khurd version there is a hint of his fearlessness, but the total view is that, on the whole, he is *not* super-normally strong.

Secondly, there is devotion to him by his pet buffalo but not devotion to the pet buffalo by Birnath. He does not show a super-normal interest in the buffaloes.

Finally, the situation which causes his death is his exposure of the seven witches. These witches are either led by his sister, pretend to be his sister, or are all his sisters. The decision to kill him is the decision of a group outside the family or the village,

> "As the lion the kine, as the wolf the sheep
> As the schoolboy drives the ball
> So trench by trench did Malkhan leap
> With his Rajputs following all.
>
> " 'If I gave thee barley in winter,
> And oil in time of rain,
> If Parmal stinted thee not of milk
> In thy foalhood lightsome and vain,
>
> " 'Kabutri, my mare, my Pigeon,
> Mine honour save this day,
> And let not thy foot take a backward step
> Whilst foes uphold the fray!'
>
> "Kabutri arched her brown neck free,
> And they rushed on the Chauhan men;
> But, where her master dealt with three,
> The mare she smote down ten.
>
> "For with teeth she tore and her heels she flung
> That she made a passage wide,
> And each howda she passed, in air she sprang,
> That her lord might reach the side."

"In India it is natural that elephants should play a role similar to that of horses. In folk-lore they betray, or serve, their masters like human beings, and even converse with them in human voice." (N. M. Penzer, op. cit., II, viii).

THE VERTICAL MAN

and with its own witch values. None the less, it involves a disguised form of brother-sister hostility and the personal element is not entirely lacking. This hostility is fundamental to the myth and the reasons for it will become clear when we consider the myth in its main form.

V

THE SECOND BRANCH LEGEND: THE QUARREL WITH THE SISTER

With the second branch legend, the exposure of the witches goes and its place is taken by Bir Kuar's quarrel with his sister.

This quarrel appears in four different forms.

In versions from Mahauli and Muhammadganj and also in certain versions of the main myth, Bir Kuar is stopped by his sister at the door of his marriage room and is asked to surrender his pet buffalo as a wedding present. Although he refuses, his sister insists. When he finds she is not open to reason, he pushes her aside and after that, she curses him.

Secondly, in a version from Dinadag his sister warns him not to take his buffaloes into the jungle at night because of the tigers in it. Bir Kuar does not do what she says and is cursed for disobeying her.

Thirdly, in a *chānchar* of Simarbari, Bir Kuar goes with his sister to milk the buffaloes but instead of milking all of them he lets the calves go when only four have been done. His sister upbraids him and Bir Kuar slaps her. A curse is not actually stated but the later remarks of Bir Kuar's mother imply that one has been given.

Finally, in a version of the main myth from Mananpur, Bir Kuar's sister finds him leaving his wife on their wedding night and going out into the jungle. She remonstrates with him but when he pays no attention, she curses him.

These versions are supplemented by two subsidiary ones. In a *chānchar* from Kauwal, Bir Kuar's mother and sister plead with him not to go into the jungle as his enemy is waiting:

20

Birnath starts from his house and his mother
Catches his waist

THE MYTH OF BIR KUAR

"Son, do not take the buffaloes into the jungle
In the jungle your enemy waits"
But he does not listen.
He goes a short way and his sister
Stops him
"Brother, do not take the buffaloes into the jungle
In the jungle your enemy waits"
To their pleading he does not listen
And goes into Brindaban.
Alone in the jungle
He came on a tiger
He folded his hands but the tiger
Sprang
He killed it
Then down on it, into it, he pressed his buttocks
He killed the tiger and down on it
Into it he pressed his buttocks.
On the scene the tigress comes
And is wild with grief
Who has killed my mate in the jungle
And is stamping him with his buttocks?[1]
So strong is the tigress that
She hurls Birnath from him
Holds him and wrenches his head off
In the jungle she leaves his body
And where the cows are tied
She tosses the head.
Parai his buffalo
Wanders in the jungle
And with the body she comes home
His mother and sister, seeing it,
Begin to cry bitterly
"He did not heed what we said
He has met the tiger"
Placing his corpse on the ground, his sister
Put up an image

[1] Havelock Ellis has recorded a number of examples drawn from the West and the East illustrating the use of the buttocks as a mark of contempt. (*Studies in the Psychology of Sex*, V, 100–101.)

62 THE VERTICAL MAN

"All in the world will see it
And seeing, will remember him."

In the second version, from Babhantalao tola of Rohtas, Bir
Kuar's wife pleads with him not to go into the jungle because it
is night. In neither case are their pleadings of any avail, and
although they do not curse him, he goes away, leaving them
resenting his behaviour.

THE DEMAND FOR THE WEDDING PRESENT

The version which makes the refusal of a wedding present the
cause of disaster is current in Muhammadganj. According to this
legend, "On the day of Birnath's *gaunā* or the consummation of
his marriage, his sister stopped him at the bridal chamber and
demanded a buffalo named Barowa as her present. Barowa and
Banda were Birnath's head and pet buffaloes. Birnath refused
to give her Barowa. They quarrelled and Birnath pushed her
aside and went into the room. His sister cursed him that a tiger
would kill him.

One afternoon Birnath was grazing his buffaloes in the jungle
when at dusk a tiger came and killed him. Banda and Barowa
reached the spot, lifted his body up and brought it home.

A carpenter who was Birnath's friend heard of his death and
hurried to Birnath's house. When he saw Birnath lying dead, he
also died.

The carpenter had a servant named Sheikh Babal who saw his
master run out of the house and thought that he would lose his
days' wages. So he also ran after him but tripped up on a stone
and died from the fall.

After his death, Birnath appeared in a dream to his castemen
(the Kishnaut Ahirs) and told them to put up pairs of posts and
worship him and the carpenter. Since then they have received
joint worship. In the same dream, Sheikh Babal also appeared
and asked for a share in the worship. For this reason a small
offering is put aside for him. The posts are known as Bir Kuar—
Bir is Birnath and Kuar is the carpenter."

In this version, although it is the sister's curse which causes his
death, it is Bir Kuar's devotion to his pet buffalo which is the

THE MYTH OF BIR KUAR 63

overriding element in the situation. This element is elaborated in other versions to which we will come later but at this stage we may note that although Bir Kuar's reaction is violent, it is his sister's action which is aggressive, and Bir Kuar is not without reason in refusing her demand. In view of this refusal, his sister becomes a disappointed girl, but in view of the curse, Bir Kuar becomes a wronged man. His death therefore is not his fault, but is rather a necessary part of the whole situation. It means that however Bir Kuar might have acted, he is bound to be killed. The whole situation has become fatal for him and what actually kills him is not his sister's pettiness but his love for his buffaloes. To this I shall return later.

THE COMMAND TO AVOID THE JUNGLE AT NIGHT

I. *The Dinadag Legend*

If in the preceding version, the sister's curse results from a conflict of claims, in the next version it is the spurning of her advice which leads to Birnath's death.

In this version, "Birnath untied his buffaloes one night and took them to the jungle to graze. His mother told him not to take them as there were many tigers and tigresses. But he did not listen and took them to the jungle. When he had gone a little way, his sister came after him and told him not to take them. But again he did not listen. When his sister saw that he was not heeding her, she cursed him that a blind tigress would come and kill him. A blind tigress then came and mauled him. Birnath's buffalo, Paraiya, came and killed the tigress. She then put Birnath on her back and took him to the village. As they were nearing the village, Birnath told her to put him near the tethering ground and to call his friends and castemen. Paraiya did so. A carpenter, a Rajput and a Musalman who were his friends, came. When they saw that Birnath was dying, they also died. After his death, Birnath appeared in a dream to his family and told them to put up posts in the tethering place and worship him."

Here, the emphasis begins to shift. Bir Kuar's sister and mother cease to be petty and are merely solicitous for his welfare. Bir

64 THE VERTICAL MAN

Kuar ceases to be the wronged man and becomes the foolhardy one. At the same time, the sister's curse ceases to be what really kills him. The blind tigress is already waiting when Bir Kuar disregards the warning, and the curse simply describes the existing situation and does not add to it. It is again the devotion of Bir Kuar to his buffaloes which makes the situation fatal.

Minor points which should be stressed are:

It is not a tiger but a tigress, and not simply a tigress, but a blind tigress which kills him.

The killing is automatic and there is no suggestion that Bir Kuar is abnormally strong. The emphasis is on the man with the obsession—not on the man with the strength.

Three mysterious friends—the carpenter, the Rajput and the Musalman—again gather for his death and do not survive the shock.

2. *The Babhantalao legend*

This pre-existing fatality is continued in the Babhantalao legend. According to this version, "Birnath and Kuar were two brothers. Birnath went to fetch his wife from his father-in-law's. As he was coming back, a witch felt a grudge against him and arranged for a tiger to kill him when he would next take his buffaloes to graze. It is not known who the witch was or why she had the grudge. On getting back, Birnath went to the jungle to graze his buffaloes. His wife implored him not to go as it was night, but he did not listen and took his buffaloes out. A tiger then came and killed him. Birnath's ghost came on his brother Kuar asking him for his pet buffalo and crying 'Parai, Parai.' Kuar in his frenzy ordered his parents to put up a post and worship Birnath. Later, Kuar also was killed by a tiger and Birnath appeared in a dream to the Ahirs and told them to put up another post to Kuar and worship him also. Since then two posts are being made.

In this version, there are four points of major importance.

While the curse by a witch is stated to be the *prima facie* cause of Birnath's death, the account actually brushes it aside and shows it as virtually only incidental.

It is again the devotion to the buffaloes which makes Birnath insist on grazing them at night and is the real cause of his death.

25. TILAUTHU

26. ROHTAS, Bholna tola

27. RAMDIHRA

28. BARKA TIARA

29. RAMNA

30. RAMBANDH

31. NIMAHAT

32. KUSIARA

THE MYTH OF BIR KUAR

This general devotion to the herd at the same time conceals a particular passion for Parai, and the latter emerges in Birnath's cry of agony when he comes on Kuar. It is not for his mother, sister, brother or castemen that he cries, but for Parai, the pet.

There is again no emphasis on Birnath's strength.

THE REPRIMAND FOR LETTING LOOSE THE CALVES

If the passion for the pet buffalo dominates the Babhantalao legend, it is this which indirectly occasions the sister's curse in the Simarbari *chānchar*.

This *chānchar* falls into five parts:

A preliminary section praising Birnath and stating that he was born in Ayodhya and reared in Brindaban.

An episode of great tenderness in which Birnath, after fetching his wife for their second marriage, falls asleep from tiredness, but later goes out to comfort Parewa, the pet buffalo, who is crying because of his neglect.

A second episode into which the first blends and which contains the milking incident and the implication of the curse.

A scene in which Birnath, angry from his mother's alarm, stalks out into Brindaban with his buffaloes, sees Parewa suddenly attacked by a tiger, goes to her rescue, beats back the attacks of seven tigers and is finally mauled by a blind tigress.

Finally an exhortation to worship.

21

Where was the birthplace of Baba Birnath?
He was born in Ayodhya
He was reared in Brindaban
His posts are everywhere
And from his castemen he levies worship
When will my castemen come?
The hour for worship is passing
Oh a hero is Birnath
And a grazer of buffaloes
When I sing, the buffaloes return
It was the day of Birnath's *gauna*
He went for his wife

E

THE VERTICAL MAN

With his wife, he was coming
He was tired and slept.

As she was tied, his
Buffalo Parewa
Began to cry loudly.
At the breaking hour before sunrise
Birnath awoke from sleep
Birnath went out
Where the buffaloes were lying
Wiping her tears with his cloth
He told her not to cry
"Because I was tired I slept."

His sister, Radha Rukmini
Comes. She comes
For milking the buffaloes
Two or four buffaloes Birnath milked
And let loose the calves of the herd
Sister Radha Rukmini
Speaks
"You are milking only four buffaloes
And letting the calves go?
How can you hope for a living?"
Hearing this, Birnath
Flared into anger.
Sharply he slapped her
And crying she went home
His mother Kosila
Is filled with alarm.
"The curse of a mother
Can be washed by the Ganges
But the curse of a sister
Goes on."
Hearing this, Birnath
Flared into anger
Keeping the ropes on the buffaloes
He drove them to Brindaban
And squats on a hillock.

THE MYTH OF BIR KUAR 67

Suddenly a tiger
Leaps on Parewa
Birnath
Drives it away
Driving it away a second comes
Driving away the second a third comes
Driving away the third, a fourth comes
Driving away the fourth, a fifth comes
Seven tigers he drives away
And when they had gone a blind tigress
Rips his belly.

Baba Birnath calls to his castemen
"Listen, my castemen,
Settle some *chamārs* to the south of the village
And on the middle night of Kartik
And the last day of Kartik
Worship me
And free of fee, the *chamārs* will beat their drums
There Birnath gives his castemen peace."

Here the following points arise:

Birnath's marriage duties again weigh like a feather on him
and the grand passion is again for Parewa. He begins to talk to
her as if she were his mistress.

In the milking incident, Birnath is interested less in the milk
than in being kind to the calves. He acts, in fact, as if his function
were not to earn his living by the buffaloes but to nurture them
as petted animals. His view of them is entirely non-economic.

His anger at having his view doubted is almost hysterical,
because his view is now based on what amounts to a religious
intuition—an intuition, that is, which is no longer based on
normal values.

Finally he is again the supernormally strong man for whom
the female—the blind tigress—proves completely fatal.

THE VERTICAL MAN

THE REPRIMAND FOR REFUSING TO SLEEP WITH HIS WIFE

The Mananpur chānchar[1]

This *chānchar* contains almost all the main elements of the myth but it will complete the analysis of the sister's curse if I summarize the relevant part here.

According to this poem, Birnath had no sooner brought his wife home for consummating his marriage than he picked up his stick and ran to his buffaloes to take them to the jungle. His mother and father implored him to spend the night with his wife but he brusquely disregarded them. His sister then went to him and insisted that at least on his wedding night he must sleep with his wife. Birnath threw her down and she then cursed him that if he went into Brindaban, the starving witch tiger would get him.

In this particular form, Paraiya, the pet buffalo, is absent and it is a generalized enthusiam for the herd which drives him out into the jungle. The buffaloes are now an obsession which overrides all other considerations and against which his wife, father, mother and sister remonstrate in vain. The extreme form has been reached, for the wife is of less importance than the herd.[2]

[1] See poem 25.

[2] The possibility of this fateful development is sometimes accepted and even praised by Ahirs. The Ballad of the Buffaloes of Gaura, for example, celebrates two Ahirs of the Central Provinces who spurn their mother and leave all for the sake of their buffaloes:

When they saw the boys, the she-buffaloes embraced them.
Weeping, weeping, the she-buffaloes talked to them.
When they heard the story, Chaura and Makunda went to their mother.
They folded their hands and said to her, "O mother,
The buffaloes our father grazed have come.
We will go to graze them now."
"O sons, your father died while caring for them.
My sons, do not go, listen to your mother."
O Ragi, the mother grew weary persuading them.
Chaura and Makunda went to care for the buffaloes.
The leader of the herd blessed Chaura and Makunda
O Ragi, from that day the Mirchuk sits on cows and buffaloes.
Chaura and Makunda grew up daily.
The Raja of Mahar got very poor.
By the curse of the buffaloes the Raja lost his wealth.

THE MYTH OF BIR KUAR

THE UNSPECIFIED QUARREL

Finally, it is in a vague, unspecified quarrel that the brother-sister hostility is clinched. According to the legend which I heard in Tumba, "Bir Kuar was a very strong Ahir who was always grazing his cattle and could even lift his buffaloes and cows in his arms. He thought that there was no one who could equal him in strength. But a woman envied him his power and cursed him, saying that she would make him wither away. Bir Kuar became thinner and thinner and at last he died. As he was dying, he said that all Ahirs who had cattle should worship him."

This version is obviously summary, but it is not unimportant for it emphasizes the aspect of Bir Kuar as the super-normally strong man, the fact that he exults in his buffaloes, and that his death is due to a hostile woman whose will destroys him.

SUMMARY : THE SECOND BRANCH

The stages reached in the second branch may be summarized as follows:

Victory to Chaura and Makunda who made the Ahir race to flourish. (Verrier Elwin, *Folk-songs of Chhattisgarh* (Bombay, 1946), 296.)

The overriding importance of the buffaloes is stressed in yet another *chanchar* from the Bir Kuar country.

"Husband, sell the buffalo and buy a brown cow. Then you will have a pair. Graze the cows during the day-time and tether them at sunset. The buffalo is like a co-wife to me. It wakes you and takes you from me when you are sleeping. The cows you have only to graze all day and tether at sunset. All night you sleep heavily with clasped arms and no sooner is day breaking than you run and loose the buffalo."

"Wife, I will sell the mother of my house and pair my buffalo."

"Husband, if you sell the mother of your house to install another buffalo who will bring you food and the wooden slab for washing? Who will serve your food hot? Who will rub you with oil? Who will nod to you when you talk?"

"A maid will bring me water and the wooden slab for washing. My sister will serve my food hot. My mother will rub me with oil. The buffalo will nod to me as I talk."

"Husband, your mother will die and leave you. Your sister will go to her husband. Your maid will work in another family. You will live alone."

"Wife, if my mother dies, if my sister goes to her husband, if the maid works in another's family, I will sell the buffalo, and, taking a sadhu's gourd and a stick, I will go to a strange land."

70   THE VERTICAL MAN

Unlike the first branch, Birnath tends to be treated as a strong man. In the quarrels with his sister, he is almost always in the wrong.

There is devotion to him by his pet buffalo and this is more than reciprocated by him. Indeed his passion for her amounts to an obsession which sweeps away all other interests and duties. Birnath is now the man whose super-normal interest is his buffaloes.

The situation which causes his death is the sister's quarrel and her curse. But just as in the first branch the witches incident transmits the brother-sister hostility, in the second branch the brother-sister quarrel transmits a more fundamental situation. This is the conflict between the claims of the family and the claims of the herds—the love of the buffaloes and the love of the wife.

VI

THE MAIN MYTH

I now turn to the main myth. This is contained in three poems and one account. Of the poems two are alternative versions from Baknaur, the third is from Mananpur, while the account was collected in Ramna.

THE BAKNAUR VERSIONS

The first of these *chānchars* begins with a recital of some preliminary details. It states that Birnath was born at twilight in the month of *Magh* and that his *chhat* ceremony took place on the sixth day. In his tenth year, he was married in Tirhut garh and on completing his twelfth year, he burst into his youthful powers. When he was sixteen, his *gaunā* took place. The poem then proceeds.

22

March saw the *gaunā* of Birnath
Coming in the *gaunā*, Birnath
Waited at the door
Dewaki, sister of Birnath

THE MYTH OF BIR KUAR

Stood in his way at the door
"You are my only brother
Give me the buffalo I choose."
Birnath said:
"Listen, Dewaki sister
Three hundred and sixty are the buffaloes
Take which you like
But leave Parai."
Dewaki said:
"Listen, until I get
Parai I stay at your door."
Hearing this, Birnath grew sulky
"Three hundred and sixty buffaloes, sister, you leave!
Not a single one pleases you?
Parai you shall not have
Whether you go or stand."

Pushing her, Birnath
Enters the bridal chamber
And makes ready for sleep.
For loosing the buffalo, Parai, the time came
Parai is shaking her bell: Baba Birnath
Suddenly wakes
Loosing the ropes he sees
Seven lamps. What are these
Seven lamps?
Clever in witchcraft was
Dewaki sister of Birnath
With her seven girls she was
Revelling
Stripped of their clothes
And dancing in girdles of brooms
Into the jungle where the lights were
He takes Parai his buffalo
Into the jungle where the lights were
The buffalo falters at going
Birnath sees the lights
And goes where the lights are

THE VERTICAL MAN

The seven lamps of the witches were burning
Merrily the witches were dancing
Birnath comes on their clothes
Taking the clothes he goes
Back to his buffalo.

The dance of the witches
Ends and they look for their clothes
None of them finds them
Then Dewaki says:
"Listen, the bell which is sounding
Is the bell of Birnath.
He it is who has taken our clothes."
Over to Birnath troop the seven witches
And they stand before him
Dewaki speaks to him:
"Listen my brother
At stake is the honour of the village
This once give us back our clothes."
Birnath returns the clothes
And the witches cover their bodies.

Going a little way the witches
Confer together
"Listen.
Dawn will bring Birnath home
And the news will spread in the village." The witches
Confer together
Each of them
Summons a scorpion
Each of the seven scorpions
Birnath kills
Dewaki knows this by magic
"Listen. Birnath is living."
Each of the witches
Sends a snake
Each of the seven snakes
Birnath kills
Dewaki knows it by magic, and the witches

THE MYTH OF BIR KUAR

Send seven tigers
Six of the tigers
Birnath kills
But a blind tigress
Lurked in a bush
From killing the tigers,
Birnath was coming
When the blind tigress
Sprang
Bitten by the tigress Birnath fell
Birnath was dying
At the breaking hour before sunrise
The buffaloes moved to the *bathan*
All of the buffaloes passed
None of them lifted up Birnath

Last of them Parai his buffalo comes
Seeking her master
And finding him dying
With her teeth she lifts him
And she carries him home
To the house of his mother
At the door his mother
Is beating her breasts
Birnath speaks:
"Listen, my mother."
Birnath speaks:
"Listen, my mother
On the edge of the village
Put up my posts
Put on them my image
Tell my castemen to
Worship me."

In the second *chānchar* there is a change of order. Instead of the witch incident being the immediate means through which the curse comes to its fatal conclusion, the sister's quarrel clinches the witch incident and is followed by the death in the jungle.

THE VERTICAL MAN

23

Gone is the night the first quarter
Gone is the last quarter
At the hour when waking the birds sing
At the breaking hour before sunrise
Birnath his buffaloes loosened
Birnath to Brindaban took them
Morning found Birnath in Brindaban
Seven witches were in the midst of their revels
Birnath their dresses collected
Birnath removed their clothes
Finished their magic, the witches:
"What man is he who has taken our clothes?"
Dewaki sister of Birnath
Asks for the clothes
"Baba, our clothes to go home, our clothes
To save your honour."
Birnath returned the clothes
Taking her clothes, the sister of Birnath
Planned to avenge.

Meanwhile his *gaunā* was fixed
Birnath his bride was bringing
Home to his house
Blocking the bridal room, the sister of Birnath
Stood in the way
"Give me your buffalo, Parai,
And then I will let you in."
"Take which you will of my buffaloes
Take of the three hundred and sixty
But Paria I will not give,"
Birnath grew angry from standing
And pushing his sister he entered
"Baba Birnath by the time
Your yellow *dhoti* has faded,
You will turn to ashes
And be blown in the wind."
Seven tigers sent Dewaki
Seven tigers Birnath belaboured

THE MYTH OF BIR KUAR

And they fled to their dens
Birnath six tigers slaughtered
The seventh, the blind tigress, killed Birnath
To the three hundred and sixty called Birnath
"Give me a little milk, my buffaloes
Now I am dying."
Parai his buffalo gave him
A jet of her milk
Birnath lay down to die
Three hundred and sixty his buffaloes
Stayed as they were
Birnath was lifted by Parai
Taking him, taking him Parai
Brought him, brought him to his mother's
There Birnath's body, Birnath's body was burnt
There Birnath said
"All of you who are present
Put up my posts
Worship me."[1]

THE MANANPUR VERSION

In this *chanchar*, also, the legend starts with Birnath's second marriage but there is no demand for Parai. Instead, as soon as he reaches home, Birnath deserts his wife and runs to his buffaloes.[2]

[1] Baknaur p.s. Rohtas.

[2] In the Chhattisgarh song, "The Ballad of Lorik and Chandaini," neglect of a wife for the cattle also characterizes the Ahir cult hero, Lorik.

The brave Bir Bawan milked the two-and-fifty cows and drank the milk
But his friend, the Rawat, came and told him of Chandaini.
"Come, come, my brave warrior, for the day to fetch your bride has come."
"But my head is splitting with pain, my brother, I cannot go for her.
Take my horse Katar and go yourself to fetch my bride."
The Rawat takes the great horse Katar and brings the bride home;
He stands outside the house and calls to Bir Bawan.
Bir Bawan gulps down his dish of rice and belches loudly,
The noise of his belch goes for twelve kos round.
Patting his belly he comes out and prepares to milk the cows.
His bride Chandaini watches him astonished.
His bride has come and he takes no notice of her.

(Verrier Elwin, op. cit., 342)

THE VERTICAL MAN

24

Where was the birthplace of Baba Birnath, brother
And where did he marry?
Bhojpur was his birthplace
In Siris[1] he was married
His wedding and *gaunā* are over
His wife is put in the litter
And taking her with him
He started for home.
Reaching his home
He pulled out his *kusum* stick
Pulling his stick out he
Runs to his buffaloes
Seeing him running, his
Parents entreat him
"This night at least you must
Spend in your house
Wait until dawn
To go to the buffaloes."
He did not listen to his mother
He rooted out the tongue of his father.

Somewhere his sister is sitting
She goes and catches his hands
"Do as I say today, brother
Tonight at least
You must sleep at home
He throws off her hands,
And she falls down
Hurt by the fall, she
Curses him
"Step into Brindaban, Baba Birnath
And the hungry tiger will get you"
After these curses, her brother
Goes to the buffaloes
Going, he gets to them
And looses them

[1] Siris, a village in Barun police station, Gaya district.

THE MYTH OF BIR KUAR 77

Then with his *kusum* stick
He drives them to Brindaban

In Brindaban seven witches
Were in the midst of their revels
And their lamps were lighted
His eyes fell on them and
Lifting the clothes of the witches, he
Took them away
Lifting the clothes of the witches, and
Taking them with him, he
Went with his buffaloes
When the revels were over each witch
Began to search for her clothes
None of them finds them the witches
Say to each other
"The bell of Birnath is sounding in the jungle
If you like, sisters
You may go naked before him
And appeal to his pity
Either he wants to undo us, sisters
Or safely he will send us home"
All the witches go over
And fall at his feet
"Our honour is also your honour, brother
Give us back our clothes"
To all the witches, Birnath
Returns the clothes
They wear them and whisper together
"Listen, sisters
If now you go home
Birnath will have you killed
There is no help but to
Put the witch tiger on him"
Called by the witches, the witch tiger
Springs at Birnath
Seven days and nights
With the *kusum* stick
Birnath beats it

THE VERTICAL MAN

But on the seventh the stick
Split,
Birnath
Climbs a *kusum* tree
As he climbs, the tiger
Climbs after him
The tiger climbs
The tiger climbs into the tree
Up in the tree the tiger kills him

In a dream Baba Birnath said
"Whoever is my casteman
Should put up a post to me
If you put up my posts
I shall show kindness to the buffaloes
If you put up my posts,
I shall show kindness to the cows"
All his castemen are putting up posts
And to the cattle Baba Birnath is kind.

THE RAMNA ACCOUNT

According to this legend, "Birnath was bringing his wife home for their second marriage when his sister stopped him at the bridal chamber and demanded the buffalo Paraiya as her wedding present. Birnath said she might have any other buffalo but not that one. She insisted and would not be satisfied with any other. Birnath refused to give up Paraiya, and started to go with his wife into the room. His sister cursed him saying 'As you have disappointed me, so my sister-in-law will be disappointed of her wedding night.' As he crossed the threshold of the room he heard the bell of Paraiya and went back to attend to her saying that his *didi*, his auntie, was calling him. He then went and unloosed her and took her towards Brindaban. In the jungle he saw seven witches—a Kumhain, Rajputin, Telin, Kayasthin, Ahirin Bamhani and a Chamain—all practising witchcraft. He crept up and took away their clothes. When they had finished they found their clothes gone and hearing the bell of Birnath's buffalo they said that Birnath must have taken them. They went in the

THE MYTH OF BIR KUAR 79

direction of the bell and asked Birnath to give the clothes back. He agreed but said that they must teach him witchcraft. While the witches were teaching him they thought that if they taught him all their art, they would put themselves in his power, so they reserved one of their spells and taught him all their methods except one. When Birnath had gone, they thought that he would spread the scandal of their being witches in the village, so they decided to kill him. They therefore sent a snake, a tiger, a bear, a leopard, a hyena and two other animals. Birnath killed them all. The Kumhain, who was blind, then sent a tiger, and when the tiger came on Birnath, Birnath struck it with his stick. But the stick broke and the tiger pounced on him. Paraiya came and butted the tiger off, but not before Birnath had been mauled. She then took him on her back and as he reached home Birnath told his mother to put up posts with carved figures on them and to do him worship at Sohrai and instruct his castemen.''

VII

CONCLUSION

The versions given in the preceding section I have called the main myth because they take the two branches and fuse them into a single structure. But they do not finally resolve the fluctuating roles of Bir Kuar and his sister. At most it can be said that they incline to the view that Birnath was the truly strong Ahir obsessed with a passion for his buffaloes and dying because of it. We should not, however, be understanding the myth if we treated this as the final or the only view, for without the variations already noted it would lose much of its validity and force.

The importance of the myth is seen when we regard it as the expression of certain Ahir needs and perceptions—if we regard it, in fact, as a commentary on the whole caste situation.

This situation may be summarized as follows:

The prosperity of the caste hinges on the welfare of their buffaloes. This can be ensured by the caste faithfully tending them but there will always be crises when, owing to fertility failures, the herds are not increasing. Against these crises, it is necessary to have a form of insurance, and the only possible form is a cattle-god, whose function is to stimulate fertility.

THE VERTICAL MAN

There are, however, two other and equally important elements. Even if the herds are duly increasing, the caste will not prosper unless the Ahirs work hard, are fearless in the jungle and are strong and active. A model of the truly strong man, the true Ahir, becomes essential..

Finally, although the need to tend the buffaloes long and patiently is fundamental, it is equally vital that the means of livelihood should never become the whole of living. The herds must never be allowed to replace the family, and there must be a lesson to ensure that the buffalo is never regarded as more important than the wife.

The importance of the myth of Bir Kuar is that it takes these three diverse elements and through its varying forms projects a figure who resolves the three in himself. Bir Kuar is, at once, the fertilizer god, the model and the lesson.

The fertilizer god.—The part of the myth which qualifies him for his fertility function is precisely the part which would otherwise seem abnormal and mysterious—the relation with the pet buffalo. This relation is never depicted as sexual but it has all the appearance of a sexual passion. When Birnath goes to Parai after he has overslept, he comforts her as if he has neglected a mistress. When Birnath brings his wife, he refuses to sleep with her and instead goes at once to Parai. Similarly, on Parai's side, there is a love which makes her jingle her bell to bring her lover running, which makes her fight for and protect Birnath and finally bear him home when he is dying. At the same time, Dewaki's role is always that of the jealous spectator, the person who wants to separate two lovers. It is to prevent them coming together that she demands Parai as her present, and also implores Birnath to stay at home on his wedding night. She exhibits all the hostility of a woman who finds a member of the opposite sex turning to other and abnormal channels.

The importance of this will be obvious, for if the buffaloes are to be properly fertilized, there is no more obvious way than through a sexual relation with them. Birnath becomes the god of the buffaloes because he is obsessed with them. He acquires the power to bring the she-buffaloes on heat because he has loved one of them.

But a passion for buffaloes is of no avail unless it is linked to

33. DINADAG

34. SONBARSA

35. KUSAHAR

36. KALAPAHAR

37. ROHTAS, Bholna tola

38. RAMGARH

39. RAMGARH

40. ROHTAS, Bhabhantalao tola

THE MYTH OF BIR KUAR 81

supernatural power. Bir Kuar has first to be a god before he can be a fertilizer. This has therefore to be demonstrated, and the myth does so in the following way.

We have seen that although in many versions Birnath is shown as the super-normally strong man, this is not always the case and he is sometimes shown as being easily killed. We have also noticed that there is no uniformity in the methods by which he is shown as demanding worship. It is sometimes on his death bed, sometimes in a dream, or sometimes through the act of possessing a person. Finally, in certain versions the news of his death causes other persons immediately to die. All of these variations are important for they make it clear that Birnath was an *avatar* or incarnation. It is not his death through a tiger which makes him a god. Neither is it the dream sanction or the act of possession. He is already a god and whether he is strong or weak is irrelevant. It is through the variety of his possible deaths and qualities that the myth reveals his godhead.

The model.—But although certain versions minimize Birnath's strength, the majority show him as the truly strong man—the man who fearlessly goes through the jungle at night, who is tireless in tending the buffaloes, and who meets and defeats tigers. As such, he represents the ideal Ahir—the one who will most nearly fulfil all that the caste occupation demands of him.

The lesson.—Finally, the lesson; for if the buffalo obsession fits him for the task of fertilizer god, it is the same obsession which ruins him as a man. It is the necessity of this contradiction which the myth is designed to indicate, and it is because it is recognized as a form of diverting and sublimating sex, that the obsession is presented in the form of a brother-sister hostility.

Bir Kuar's sister represents the claims of Ahir women—the demands of the home on the breadwinner—the wife's sexual claims on her husband. This is recognized as fundamental by the caste and although Bir Kuar flouts it, he cannot avoid the consequences. The tigress who kills him is both literally and symbolically his sister who summarizes in herself the resentment of the female members of the caste. She is blind because in flouting the family sentiment Bir Kuar is outraging what is fundamental for the caste way of life and from this there is no escape and no reprieve.

F

Chapter Four

WOOD AND STONE

I

A GAINST the background of this myth, certain aspects of the sculpture will now be obvious. But before we turn to a last analysis, we have still to explain why the caste hero should have required such sculpture at all. We have seen how in the myth, Bir Kuar tells his castemen, the Ahirs, to put up a pair of wooden posts and after that, to worship him. It is always posts that he prescribes and although one style of sculpture is in stone, this is not referred to in the myth and does not have its sanction. To return, then, to an earlier question, why should Bir Kuar demand these wooden posts and why should two styles—in wood and stone—result from this behest?

II

Within the region of the sculpture no other shrines follow this pattern but there are two parallels.

One is found in the posts which are put up by Rajputs, Kayasths and Brahmans at the death ceremony of *birkhod*. At this ceremony, which occurs on the eleventh day of mourning, a young bull is dedicated and allowed to roam free—the idea being that the roaming bull will bear away the sins of the dead man. At the same time, a post with a simplified human head is put up, as a brief memorial of the dedication. These posts are not expressions of a caste style and as they are not intended to be permanent, they are usually made with little sensibility. But in their general appearance, they afford a rough approximation to the posts of Bir Kuar.

The other parallel is found in the posts which are put beside a well or in a mango grove as witnesses to the marriage of the grove or well.[1] These posts also are usually given human heads and approximate roughly to the Bir Kuar type. Neither of these

---

[1] For descriptions of these marriages, see L. S. S. O'Malley, *Bihar and Orissa District Gazetteers: Muzaffarpur*, 36–37.

WOOD AND STONE

parallels, however, does more than supply a visual analogy; for the posts of Bir Kuar neither commemorate the offering of a bull nor indicate a symbolic marriage. On the contrary, they are the simple expression of a religious command—the demand made by Bir Kuar at his death that posts should be put up.

Side by side with this insistence on posts goes the part played by a carpenter in the legends and worship. The fullest expression in a legend is the Muhammadganj version in which a carpenter is Birnath's friend who hurries to the scene of his death and dies at finding him dead. Birnath then appears in a dream, tells his castemen to put up pairs of posts, and directs them to accord joint worship both to him and the carpenter. The posts in Muhammadganj have since been known as Bir Kuar—Bir indicating Birnath and Kuar the carpenter.

This legend is the only version which expresses a sensitive relation involving equal parity, but in Dinadag the legend confirms that a carpenter, a Muhammadan, and a Rajput hurried to the scene and died on realizing that Birnath was dead, while the Dinadag worship stresses the peculiar relation between Birnath and the carpenter, by including the carpenter's offering in the offering to Birnath. Similarly in Dumarichati where Bir Kuar appears in the multiple form of a group of seven Kuars, one of the Kuars, Bishun Kuar, is identified with a carpenter, Bishwa Karma, and is worshipped as if he were an Ahir like the rest. Elsewhere a carpenter figures in summary legends as either a companion of Bir Kuar who was killed along with him and a Muhammadan (Madhkupia and Bankheta) or as a friend who also receives an offering (Bahiar Khurd). In Dhoba the carpenter friend again bears the name of Bishwa Karma.

This merging of the carpenter in Birnath is carried over to the worship and a sensitive relation is again established. In villages by the Rohtas hills, a carpenter's adze is used for executing the goat while in villages of Hussainabad *thana*, a carpenter is especially brought in for doing the execution. In Sonbarsa the carpenter who does the beheading must also be of the same family as the carpenter who made the posts.

If we examine this strange connection against the legendary background of the caste we shall find that the person of Viswa Karma is the clue to the posts. A legend of Viswa Karma is that

84 THE VERTICAL MAN

he was a Brahman who married the daughter of an Ahir.[1] By her he had nine sons who became the ancestors of various artisan castes such as Lohars, Sonars, Kaseras, and Barhis (carpenters). He is in fact a Brahman who unites the carpenters to the Ahirs by an Ahir marriage. If then we are to expose the reasons for the posts, we must see them as the expression of a sensitive caste relation. The carpenter friend is a symbol of the caste connection and the posts symbolize the interaction of the two castes.

III

If these circumstances explain the initial demand for posts, they throw no light, however, on the emergence of sculpted figures or the development of styles in stone and wood. We have seen, however, that in certain versions of the legend, Bir Kuar demands that the posts should bear his features. A carved figure has therefore the sanction of myth and the construction of a figure to represent Bir Kuar himself is thus an obvious offshoot from the first demand. Once the modified demand was publicized, we must assume that it spread within the region until it came to be regarded as the only form acceptable to Bir Kuar. The figure that represented the god in this way replaced the bleak, inhuman post that merely memorialized his death.

IV

If this explains the growth of sculpture, why then in certain areas should stone have ousted wood?

The style in wood is obviously sustained by the original command of Bir Kuar to put up posts. To many Ahirs, wood is the traditional ancestral form and any departure is not only incorrect, but wrong. Moreover, to a few, wood is an augury of good while stone is inauspicious. In general Hindu belief there is no basis for this division but once a small community has come to feel that certain objects are auspicious and others inauspicious the distinction acquires an irrational force. Finally to some Ahirs, as for instance those of Rohtas Kila, the very impermanence of wood is a reason for its maintenance. When I was discussing this with them in 1938, they said that the decay of wooden images

[1] R. V. Russell and Hira Lal, op. cit., IV, 121.

WOOD AND STONE   85

forced them to renew them at least once every ten years, that this kept the cult alert and alive and nourished in them a lively sense of their duties. To replace the wooden forms with stone would be to dismiss the cult and deaden its urgency.

In spite of these factors, however, a style in stone developed, and there are four factors which seem to have assisted its development. In the first place, although the impermanence of wood is sometimes felt to be an added merit, it is easy to see how in other places this can well have been a weakness. In the Turki tola of Daranagar where a stone image was put up in 1936 the Ahirs said that none of the harder woods were obtainable near the village and the sal wood posts which they had formerly put up were eaten every year by white ant. They had eventually grown weary of installing posts every year and at last abandoned wood in favour of stone. Even where harder woods are obtainable, the life of a wooden image is rarely more than fifty years. The constant daubing of its surface with *ghi* gives it a protective coating but its isolated situation, its exposure to the pelting rain and the blistering sun, coupled with the sporadic raids of white ant make decay inevitable; and many of the older images, in fact, owe their present squat appearance to the gradual eating away of their stumps. In these circumstances a gradual abandonment of wood and a gradual drift to stone are not unnatural. Secondly, although the view that wood is ancestral is completely compulsive for many Ahirs, the alternative form of stone is felt by some to have a greater force with the god. It is as if the wooden form is the ordinary standard offering and a stone image by being a variation from the norm, and also a more stable form, is an enhancement of the gift. To put up a stone image, therefore, is not to be listless but, on the contrary, to be more devout. Moreover, as we have seen in many places, the myth exists in fragments. Where the local version contains no hint of Bir Kuar's demand for wood, stone may well have seemed an equally valid way of honouring him. If to this we add the presence of quarries in the area and the existence of small groups of stone-cutting families, it is easy to see how the possibility of supply may finally have led to a precise and vital demand. A style in stone developed because stone was available and its stability was greater than that of wood.

THE VERTICAL MAN

V

If these factors are responsible for the two styles, why then is the area of the stone images not larger? Why did the style in stone stop where it did?

In determining the area for stone, the decisive factor is the distance from the quarries. The quarries are found on the eastern and northern flanks of the Rohtas hills, in the extreme north-west corner of the cult area. Beyond the northern flank the cult vanishes, while immediately east of the hills runs the broad and glittering expanse of the river Son. During the cold weather its sandy flats can be crossed by bullocks, but during the rains, the period when the annual worship is done, it becomes a dangerously wide and swirling river. It is this which confines the style mainly to a belt of country on the west bank and although stone images occur on the east bank they are limited to a small area close to the river and within sight of its wall of cliffs. In this eastern area, the reputation of the quarries is known, the transport difficulties are not impossibly great, while the shrinkage of the jungle makes the wooden form difficult to get. But to the south of this area the quarries are only a vague name, the distance to be travelled is more than a day's march, the difficulties of transport are greater, while the presence of the jungle makes wood plentiful. The balance of advantage is therefore no longer with stone but with wood and as it reaches a radius of roughly twenty miles from the quarries, the style in stone dwindles and comes abruptly to its end.

Chapter Five

THE REGION AND THE STYLES

I

IF circumstances led to a division of material, the production of images in wood and stone did not, however, result in sculptural anarchy. On the contrary, within a range of varying idioms the sculpture is obviously an expression of a region. In place of a welter of sharply contrasting images, the figures have all a discernible common denominator. The style is of the region rather than the sculptor. What, then, is the explanation of this unified diversity?

II

A first reason is the fact that all the sculpture supplies a demand. When an Ahir wants to install an image, he asks a Barhi or Gonr to make a Bir Kuar image for him. And by a Bir Kuar image he means an image which looks approximately like other Bir Kuar images and will be recognized as such by other Ahirs. The styles, as it were, define the god, and were the styles to fluctuate unduly they would fail to satisfy the Ahir need. Once the earliest forms had been invented, therefore, the Ahir need to visualize the god in a stable way must have quickly precipitated a common style, and once the style was formed the same kind of need imposed it on the region.

But besides this subconscious pressure from the Ahirs, there are other stabilizing factors. A style would only not be regional if from a common starting-point there were a general will to break away and devise a variety of styles. But among the Gonrs and Barhis, no such will exists. It is rather what is ancestral, traditional, and existent that commands their interest and allegiance. Once the original forms had been invented, therefore, a respect for the ancestors precluded any conscious divergences and although the process of carving inevitably introduced slight distortions and each family came to stress different sets of idioms,

88 THE VERTICAL MAN

the controlling factor must throughout have been their sense of the ancestral.

III

At the present day this sense of what is traditional determines both the wood and the stone carving. Stone images are supplied from two centres—one at Ramdihra and the other at Ranjitganj. At Ramdihra Aklu Gonr and his son, Mahangu Gonr, work together, while at Ranjitganj Ram Charitra Gonr works with his nephew, Ram Prasad.

In both these centres, the will of the family is to go on repeating the formulas it learnt from its ancestors. Ram Charitra Gonr, for example, learnt his idioms from his father, and when he carves a new image it is these idioms which determine how he works.

The preparation of a pair of images falls into two parts—firstly, the choice and extraction of two stones in the hills, the transport home, the smoothing of the surface, and secondly, the actual carving.

The first stage takes two to three days and usually involves two men since no Gonr thinks it prudent to work alone in the hills. The second stage lasts about a week.

For smoothing the surface, a tool known as a *tanki* or *chirna* is first used. This is an iron wedge about nine inches long, tapering to a bluntish point. It is used in conjunction with a hammer for chipping off the first roughnesses. Occasionally an even thicker wedge or *thapi* is used. When the stone has been roughly shaped, a finer wedge is brought into play. This is known variously as a *kurbandhi*, *paurhi* or *kararna*, and is six inches long, tapering to a half-inch edge. With this tool the smoothing of the surface is completed.

When the slab is smooth the image is scratched on it in outline. A circle for the head is first traced with a pair of iron callipers, a rectangle for the torso is drawn in with the help of an iron T-square, and finally the eyes, mouth, ears, neck and legs are scratched freehand with the *kurbandhi*. When an image carries a stick or club, a line for the stick is ruled with a *kurbandhi*, the T-square being used as the ruler. The image is then carved round the outline.

THE REGION AND THE STYLES

In both these centres the construction of the outline and the process of carving round it are done according to an inherited formula. This formula must originally have been an expression of the sensibility of a particular Gonr, but as used in a Gonr centre nowadays, it is less an expression of an individual than an individual's recapitulation of a family method. The family, as it were, standardizes an image as its "house style" and the carving of new images consists of repeating the standard formula. This formula is learnt rather than copied, and although it can be analysed as the use of a certain sized circle for the head and a certain shaped rectangle for the torso, it operates more through an instinctive sense of how the family makes an image than as a conscious copying of a defined type. When Ram Charitra Gonr is making a new image, for instance, he knows if the image is coming right, not by any reference to existing images or to any notes, but by his sense of the family formula. It is this which controls the carving and which accounts for the slight but vital variations which the products of a family display.

IV

The production of wooden images is somewhat more casual as almost every village group has at least one family of Barhis or carpenters who perhaps once or twice in a lifetime make an image. But at Lateya—in the heart of the area—there is a colony of three Barhi households which is a Bir Kuar centre. One of the carpenters, Bishuni Barhi, made eight pairs of images in the last twenty-five years and supplied, among others, the villages at Lahanga, Hisag, Babhandi and Lawadag; while Baldeo Barhi made at least three pairs and supplied Kalapahar, Lawadag and Gotha.

In this centre the process of carving is as follows: The Ahir who wants the image supplies Bishuni Barhi with the wood. Bishuni then shapes it to the required proportions and cuts and chisels out the form according to the family idiom. He does not work to any notes and does not make any pencil outlines. He learnt the style from his father and it is this ancestral style which determines the way he carves.

This method of carving applies also to other Barhis, and even

THE VERTICAL MAN

those who carve a Bir Kuar post for the first time do not make any pencil notes and do not carve from a copy. The most that they do is to look at an existing post and then cut the new one according to their memory and sense of form. When Thakuri Barhi of Kauwal was making the Dinadag posts, he first looked at some other posts in the area, and after he had seen what was wanted he proceeded to make them. He did not begin *in vacuo* but carved the images according to his sense of the regional style.

Finally, there is a question of attitude, which is not without importance. Gonrs and Barhis regard themselves as artisans rather than as artists, and the production of the images as work rather than as art. Although their carving is, in fact, the expression of a private sensibility, they do not consciously or deliberately "explore their minds." Aklu Gonr, for example, when he is carving a Bir Kuar image, does not feel that he is doing anything different from what he is doing when he shapes a grinding-stone. This unconsciousness of art makes it natural for the individual to sink himself in the region, to base his carving on a traditional form rather than invent his own—to satisfy a known demand rather than to risk a new experiment. It is this which in the last analysis explains why both the styles in wood and stone are regional.

Chapter Six

WHY THE STYLES ARE WHAT THEY ARE

I

A STYLE in sculpture springs from the sensibility. This is an axiom to which any discussion of influences must constantly return. But just as the changing circumstances of his time has led Picasso to exploit different forms—to be obsessed, now with sentiment, now with abstract relations, now with surrealist images, so, in a peasant society, economics, religion, and the art consciousness stimulate or warp different types of sensibility. If then, in final analysis, we ask why the two styles are what they are, the answer must be that the needs of the cult, together with the working conditions of the sculptor, combined so to stimulate the sensibilities of the original workers that a will to vital geometry was released.

II

We have seen that, in essentials, the cult of Bir Kuar is a cult for fertilizing buffaloes, but that behind the cult and giving it its power and force is the myth of Bir Kuar. We have analysed this into two types. In the first, Bir Kuar is the abnormally strong Ahir, who grazes his buffaloes in the jungle at night and rids the jungle of its tigers. In the second, he is the doomed Ahir—the victim of a buffalo obsession which leads him to place his buffaloes above his own family and which, in the interests of the caste, makes his death a fateful necessity. It is as the strong man who dies for love of the buffaloes that he obtains his fertility power. Finally, we have seen that the original demand for posts was expanded into a demand for figures representative of Bir Kuar in all his actual power.

These ideas constitute, as it were, the Ahir demands on the sculpture—the vital types it must project if their sense of the god is to be satisfied. The first is that the type must exude a supernormal power, and after this it may stress either of Bir

92 THE VERTICAL MAN

Kuar's attributes—his vigilant defence of the herds, his kindly strength or, finally, his tragic doom. The demand is, in other words, for a style which conveys the ideas of power with vigilance, power with kindness and, finally, power with doom.

If we consider what type of style can best fulfill these needs, it is obvious that a style of vital geometry is much the most potent. The style has to show Bir Kuar as simplified into certain attributes, and without a radical simplification of forms these basic aspects would not emerge. Similarly his appearance has to be distorted to emphasize his power. For conveying this sense of power, geometric distortions are obviously suitable since it is with certain geometric forms that power is normally associated.

But besides portraying power, the style must show the power as supernormal. For this a literal style would be of little relevance since it would at most display the god as human.[1] A geometric style through the very fact that it is anti-imitational conveys the feeling of supernatural power.

If we assume, then, an initial will to vital geometry, the needs of the cult greatly favoured its release. The vital types which the styles project fulfil exactly the needs of the myth.

III

Equally from the side of economics, all the factors favour a similar release.

The economic position of the Gonrs is that of stone-cutting labourers living at a peasant level. Their main occupation is stone-cutting—the extraction of sandstone blocks from the hills and the shaping of them into paving-stones and grinding-stones. In 1938 two pairs of grinding-stones were fetching a rupee, while the price of a paving-stone ranged from one to four annas. In addition to this, Aklu Gonr of Ramdihra grew a little rice on five bighas of land which he cultivated in return for paying half the produce. He also owned two bullocks which he used for ploughing and helping in the transport of stones. The total income

---

[1] Compare the Frankish-Alemannic ivory, *Christ on the Cross* (8th–9th century A.D.) Worringer, op. cit., Plate p. 22, where the divinity of Christ is expressed through geometry.

WHY THE STYLES ARE WHAT THEY ARE 93

from all these sources did not, however, yield him more than ten rupees in a good month, and in many months it was nearer five—a scale of income just sufficient to feed and clothe a family, but little more.

Similarly, the economic position of Barhis is only that of journeymen carpenters living at a peasant level. Their main occupation is the making of posts and planks for doors, legs for string beds, ploughs, carts, chairs and the handles of hammers and mattocks. For these there is an annual rather than a monthly demand, and in any one month their incomes may be only five rupees and rise to only a little more than ten.

On to this peasant routine of life the making of the images is grafted—in the case of Barhis, as a casual isolated act occurring only once or twice in a lifetime, and in the case of Gonrs, on an average rather more than once in two years.[1] The making of the images, therefore, was at most only a casual variation in a pinched and arduous routine.

At the same time, the rewards are indefinite and meagre. The prices are religious rather than economic, and a Gonr does not think so much of selling the image as of making it as a small gesture for which he will be rewarded. Accordingly, when an Ahir wants a Gonr to make an image, he asks him to do so and gives him a small present or *bira*. A *bira* is a kind of complimentary gift for getting a piece of work started. In Ranjitganj it is usually a rupee, and in Ramdihra it is a pice and a betel-nut. The Ahir asks him how much he will take in return for making the image. The Gonr replies that it is a religious matter and he will accept up to a cow, a *dhoti*, and some cash. The Ahir then tells him the amount he will give, and the transaction is concluded on the understanding that this amount will be given when the image is delivered. In the case of Ahirs already known to the Gonr this "price" discussion is omitted as the Gonr knows he will be given a sufficient present. The talk then simply consists of the time within which the image is wanted. Similarly, in the case of

[1] Between 1928 and 1938, for example, the Ramdihra centre supplied images to Rampur, Jamuan, Rohtas Kila, Ramdihra, Kaldag, Lohardaga, and Jagarnathpur—a total of seven sets in ten years; while the Ranjitganj centre supplied Belanja, Lahiarpur, Sahaspur, Basant Bigha, and Kamalkerwa—a total of only five.

94 THE VERTICAL MAN

villages which are not too distant, there is no anxiety for the payment, and it is after accompanying the images to the site and assisting in their erection that the Gonr receives his reward. It is only in the case of distant villages and when the Ahir is a stranger that the transaction approaches a sale. On these occasions, the Ramdihra centre exacts eight rupees at the time of making over a pair of images. But even this is taken as a present and neither the Ahir nor the Gonr would refer to it as a price.

Similarly with the Barhis, the carving is regarded as religious rather than commercial. The Ahirs recognize that the Barhi must be indemnified for his time and labour, and there are certain village rates below which it is improper to pay. But the payment is made less as a payment than as a thankoffering. Equally the Barhi does not make the posts for the payment. He makes them as a duty, and even if he were paid nothing he would still have the obligation to make them if they were needed.

Within this system of ideas the actual presents given vary considerably, but none are so large as to make a Gonr or Barhi alter his routine and all represent a minimum rather than a maximum level of payment. The Gonrs, for example, received a cow, a *dhoti*, a *sāri*, and two rupees for the Sahaspur image, and a calf, a *dhoti* and a rupee for the Belanja image. In Dinadag, when two posts were put up in 1938, the Barhi was given a *dhoti* and a bull calf. In Mathurapur two posts were made by Janaki Barhi of Bank in 1938, and he received a *dhoti* and four annas. These posts were more rudimentary than the Dinadag ones. In Chapra the more usual custom is to give only two annas for two simple posts. On the other hand, in Paharia, when two posts were put up twenty-five years ago, five rupees and a *dhoti* were presented to the carpenter, while Ramnand Barhi of Bajania received a cow, a rupee and a *dhoti* when he made two posts in 1925 for an Ahir of Muhammadganj. When it is remembered that the yield of milk from a cow is very small and that its main utility is as a source of dung for fuel and progeny for plough oxen, it will be seen that these presents affected very little the general level of living.

If we now ask what relation these economic conditions have to the style, we may distinguish two causes and effects. Firstly, the arduous peasant level of living is obviously inimical to all

WHY THE STYLES ARE WHAT THEY ARE 95

that is delicate or intricate. For a minute and loving naturalism, a degree of sheltered comfort is necessary, and that is completely lacking both to Gonrs and Barhis. A coarse way of life favours on the contrary a robust form of art, and unless the imitative standards of representational art have been foisted on an area we may expect a predilection for a simple energetic style. Secondly, the lack of leisure and the general lowness of the rewards put a premium on simplification. The more representational a style the more complicated is its execution; and even if the Barhis and Gonrs wished to be representational, it is doubtful if they would have the time. What is needed rather is a way of carving which lends itself to certain easily executed idioms and also keeps close to the natural shapes of the material. For this reason, a style of vital geometry is obviously preferable to a style of intricate representation. The one can be produced as an act of intuitive knowledge; the other requires prolonged study of a model. Similarly, a style that can use the tube of a tree as the natural basis for a geometric vertical form is much more suitable than a style which needs a naturalistic preliminary. In such conditions, vital geometry is a natural definition of art.

IV

Finally, we should stress the absence of an audience educated in the canons of naturalism. The area is still remote from all art schools. The Ahirs are still very largely illiterate. They have no preconceived views on what is accurate in drawing or what is correct in perspective. Their reactions, in fact, are as spontaneous and vital as those of children in urban society or peoples living in a cultural vacuum. They are free, in fact, to accept what they like and to like what they accept. Similarly the Gonrs and Barhis are devoid of alien standards. Occasionally a Gonr may carve a naturalistic model of a Ganesh. He regards that equally as work and the difference of market and patron effectually prevents him from treating it as relevant to his images of Bir Kuar. Moreover, the series of images mounting lonely guard on the area fortifies him in his sense of style. The fact that generations of Ahirs, Gonrs, and Barhis have regarded them with approval leads him

THE VERTICAL MAN

to define art not as the duplication of nature but in terms of the actual palpable styles which he knows.

These styles grew up undisturbed by "consciousness." The Gonrs and Barhis today are only conscious that what was approved by their ancestors is valid for themselves. If a will to vital geometry was first expressed in a sculptural vacuum, it is the persistence of that vacuum which still maintains it as a style.

To a combination of all these factors we may ascribe the fact that the two styles are what they are.

41. RAMGARH

42. BARA

43. BARA

44. BANWARI

45. PANDARIA

46. JAIRAGI

47. JAIRAGI

48. KARMA, Bairia tola

APPENDIXES

THE IDENTITY OF BIR KUAR

In the preceding chapters we have analysed the qualities of Bir Kuar which influenced the styles of sculpture. It is possible for us to do this because the myth shows Bir Kuar as a separate and distinct person, while at the same time the ritual celebrates his personal power as a caste god. We have seen, however, that while within the Bir Kuar country the Sohrai festival is a feast of Bir Kuar, outside that region it is pre-eminently a festival of Krishna. There is a similar blending of the two deities in Ahir songs. I propose, therefore, to complete the picture of Bir Kuar by analysing certain Ahir poetry and to suggest a tentative conclusion.

When the myth of Bir Kuar is examined in the light of Ahir songs, two strands of material immediately become apparent—a local kind and a type deriving from the Krishna legend. The first shows Bir Kuar as an Ahir hero, whose life moves between his buffaloes and the tiger. The second merges him in Krishna. The two kinds fuse in the witch incident, where Bir Kuar in removing the clothes of the witches re-enacts Krishna taking away the clothes of the milk-maids. Bir Kuar is thus either an Ahir hero, who in course of time has fused with Krishna, or he is a fragment or extension of Krishna, who takes the form of a local Ahir.

The ways in which Bir Kuar's identity merges in Krishna's are through the geography of the myth, the names of his sister and certain ways of Ahir thought.

If we consider the geography we find that Bir Kuar's birth-place varies between Ayodhya and Bhojpur. He is reared in Brindaban, Palamau and Bhojpur. He is married either at Tirhutgarh or in Siris. He hunts in Brindaban and drinks in Ayodhya. His discovery of the witches is in Brindaban, and it is always in Brindaban that he dies. With the exception, therefore, of a few flights into Ayodhya and Bihar, the country of Bir Kuar is the country of Krishna.

Similarly, if we look at the names of Bir Kuar's sister, we find that although on one occasion she is referred to as Kani Biramdeia, on all other occasions she either bears the name of Krishna's mother, Dewaki, or the name of his wife, Radha Rukmini. Through his sister, Bir Kuar is at once Krishna's uncle and his brother-in-law.

This confusing and conflicting relationship is given a further form in the following poem:

THE VERTICAL MAN

25

Whence came Baba Birnath, brother?
And where was he reared?
Whose breast did he suck?
What milk nurtured him?
He came from the womb of Jasoda his mother
He grew up in the lap of Dewaki his aunt.
He is thus a cousin or a foster-brother of Krishna.
  Finally, in certain poems Bir Kuar and Krishna are identical.

26

Where was the birth-place of Krishna?
For whom was he an enemy?
To whom was he a joy?
Where did he cut the bamboo?
Where did he trim the flute?
Where does he play that the sound comes to Gokula
And wakes the sleeping bodies of his thousand girls?

Dewaki gave birth to Krishna
Jasoda's breast he sucked in Mathura
There he reached his youth
Born, he gives Raja Kans a foe
And frees his parents from their bonds
In Brindaban he tends the cows
And from a slim bamboo he trims a flute
High on Daulagir he plays
And the sound comes to Gokula
And thrills the sleeping bodies of his thousand girls.
The girls ask
"Who is this trader who is born in Mathura?
Whose is the voice that thrills our limbs?
Run, sisters
And let us scan his manner as we buy our things
And view his nature
What is this trader's form
And the style of his flute?
What is this flute
Which plays on our bodies?"

Their curds are ready, they start
By the Jamuna, Krishna

THE IDENTITY OF BIR KUAR 101

Is standing in a boat
The Jamuna's water is in flood
And all the girls will be drowned
Krishna is sitting like a boy
And the girls call him
To bring the boat to land
Krishna says
"What will you pay me if I bring the boat in?"
The girls reply
"A piece of bread if you're quick,"
Krishna says
"Listen. In each of your bosoms are two oranges.
Let me have them."
"My husband paid sixty rupees
And has not yet enjoyed me."
Not a girl agrees.

Krishna becomes an old man
And shifts to another ferry
The girls troop over saying
"That was a slip of a boy and we women got the better
    of him."
Krishna is sitting like an old sailor
When the girls call the boat.
He takes them all on board. He pushes off
Out in the stream
He catches their skirts and holds their wrists
He puts his fingers in their bosoms
And bruises their breasts
With all the girls he frolics
And lands them over the river.

Up to Jasoda they go
Some of them show their skirts
And some the slips that supported their breasts
"Your son has tampered with our honour
Why do you let him run so wild?"
Jasoda replies
"You were always a bad lot
And my son is no better."

THE VERTICAL MAN

27

Where was the birth-place of Birnath?
Where did he graze the *dhenua*[1] cow?
Where did he play the flute?
Where was Radhika sleeping
And the seven hundred girls
Whose bodies were thrilled?
In Brindaban he grazed the *dhenuā* cow
And puts the flute to his mouth
In Gokula sleeps Radhika
And there her body is thrilled
Who made the flute
And placed it in his mouth?
Ram made the flute
And Birnath the bold
Has put it to his mouth
And plays and thrills the girls.

At the hero's birth
All the girls were unmarried
They take the infant in their arms
And feel the contact of a lover
In their arms they dandle him
And let him smash their pots
And eat their curds
They tell Jasoda how wild the boy is
And how he tampers with them
Jasoda says he is only a baby six months old
And is sound asleep on the quilt
What wicked lies they are telling
Mother Jasoda hides
And herself sees him
Throwing their pots down and rumpling their skirts.
"Three hundred and sixty girls
Have yet to be married in Gokula
And I will daub them all with the scarlet"
The girls upbraid Jasoda
"He has stained us all with scarlet
On all the three hundred and sixty of us
He has put the mark of the married."

[1] See glossary.

THE IDENTITY OF BIR KUAR 103

All the girls go up the mountain
All the girls go up to worship the gods
All the girls hunt for the boy god
And to worship him they climb the mountain
On the mountain they go and they say
"The boy is alone. Where are his parents?" They say
"How calm must his parents be"
On the way up the mountain
The boy frolics
He climbs the mountain and the girls
Climb after to get to him
"If your father came
He would lift the mountain on his hand."

When we scrutinize these poems we are confronted with a remark-
able identity, for just as Krishna in Poem 26 plays the flute and thrills
the sleeping girls, Birnath also plays the flute and thrills the girls.
Equally, just as Krishna in Poem 26 romps with the milk-maids,
Birnath in Poem 27 rumples their skirts. In the two poems the
characters are identical and it is only the names which differ.

There is a similar confusion in the following poem.

28

I come for Birnath
How should I describe him?
On one side a cobra hisses
And on the other hisses Nag
On his throne Birnath hisses
And vanquishes the foe
Sweetly sings the *suiya*
Shrilly calls the partridge
Birnath asks in anger
Who has started the dance of the cows?
Many as the stars are the cows of Krishna
Your cowherd, Krishna, sets the cows to dance.

In this poem the question is asked by Birnath, but the reply is
addressed to him as Krishna. In these poems, Birnath and Krishna
fuse. Birnath is no longer the uncle or the brother-in-law, the cousin
or the foster-brother. He is Krishna himself.

It does not seem possible to say which of these two elements is
prior—whether Bir Kuar was actually a caste ancestor who was later

104 THE VERTICAL MAN

expanded into Krishna or whether he originated as a form of Krishna who was peculiarly relevant to Ahir needs. Either is equally possible. One of Krishna's characteristics in *The Ocean of Love* is his flexibility—his power to appear in different forms, and there is, therefore, nothing improbable in the Kishnaut Ahirs stabilizing one of his forms as their caste deity. Equally there is nothing impossible in the deified hero evolving into a form of Krishna, in the Ahirs believing that one of their apparent ancestors was, in fact, a form of Krishna. All that is clear is that in present Ahir thought Bir Kuar is no longer simply a deified hero, neither is he merely a caste ancestor. His functions as fertilizer-god, as model and lesson remain distinct, but some, at least, of his aura of romantic power derives from his identification with the major deity.

THE ROLE OF THE GODLINGS

I

THE LAME MAN

We have seen that in the course of worshipping Bir Kuar, the Ahirs make offerings to a number of mysterious figures.[1] These acts of supplementary worship do not obviously influence the sculpture, yet they are not without significance for the cult. If, therefore, we are to understand the ritual in all its intricate variety, we must attempt to remove the mystery which surrounds these odd associates.

Among these minor figures, the name which bulks largest in the worship is that of the lame man, Langru Bir. It is in his name that the pantomime of lameness is performed, and it is he who almost always receives an extra offering. But the name is charged with ambiguity. There is no version of the main myth which refers to it, and in the substitute legends his identity wavers from village to village. Sometimes Langru Bir is Bir Kuar's brother, sometimes an unknown associate, sometimes a servant. In isolated villages he is a *begar* or fag, and he even fuses with the Pathan servant of the landlord and with the carpenter. He is sometimes a Muhammadan, sometimes a carpenter and sometimes an Ahir, and the form he takes changes with every village. Only in the character of lameness is he constant.

This obscure multiplicity of roles suggests that he is not a separate person but an aspect of Bir Kuar himself, and there are two circumstances which support this interpretation.

In the first place, although almost all the main legends refer to a fight between Birnath and a tigress, there is no common formula for the way in which he died. He is either killed outright or he suffers a delayed death. In the latter case, he is mauled but not killed and it is his buffaloes that carry him home. The nature of this mauling is glossed over in most of the legends, but in one, the Tardih version, it is made clear that Bir Kuar was mauled in the leg. It is this laming which in the worship takes the form of the lame man, dramatizing a version of Bir Kuar's death and emphasizing his collapse into godhead. Just as Eve is the rib of Adam, the lame man is the leg.

Secondly, although the phase of the medium's ecstasy during which he hobbles like a lame man is usually referred to as the phase of Langru Bir, it almost always plays the role of dispelling Bir Kuar. Thus in Lawadag, when the medium is pushed down, the pushing down

[1] See pp. 32–35.

106   THE VERTICAL MAN

signifies not that Langru Bir has left him but that Bir Kuar has left, and this closes the worship. Similarly, in villages where the medium throws a stick, it is Bir Kuar and not Langru Bir who is dislodged. Summing up the process, we might say that during the ecstasy it is Bir Kuar who is throughout present and who works on the medium, and that the concluding stage re-enacts his fatal lameness. The different person is merely the label for the different stage.

Finally, as we have seen in the Khajuri version, the medium representing Bir Kuar mounts on an Ahir who represents Langru Bir. The lame man hobbles with him and then collapses, and with this collapse the *pujā* ends and Bir Kuar leaves the medium. This is a vivid diagram of Bir Kuar's death. The medium merging with the lame man is Bir Kuar sinking into lameness. The collapse is the death of the lame Bir Kuar and the end of the ecstasy is his elevation into a god.

II

THE STRANGE MUHAMMADAN

A second figure who, like Langru Bir, plays no part in the main myth but who constantly recurs in the worship is a Muhammadan. He is sometimes a friend of Birnath, sometimes a Muhammadan cowherd, and sometimes the Pathan servant of a landlord. In isolated villages he takes the form of a Khan Sahib, a Muhammadan dealer in bangles, the Muhammadan servant of the carpenter, a Jolaha servant, and a nameless Pathan. Finally, in various villages, he assumes the name of Gopi Mian and in others he fuses with Langru Bir.

Of these forms the only one with a precise and widely diffused legend is the Pathan servant of the landlord. According to this legend the Ahirs had collected all the village milk for doing Birnath's worship when the Pathan servant of a Muhammadan landlord came and demanded milk. The Ahirs then placed all the milk before him and told him he might take it away if he could. The Pathan was taking it when a tiger came and killed him. As he died, he said that the Ahirs must worship him.[1]

A Tardih variant brings the legend nearer to Birnath's lifetime. According to this the milk was demanded from Birnath's brother, Kuar, who declined to give it on the ground that it was needed for Birnath's *pujā*. The Muhammadan insisted and then there was a quarrel, in the course of which Kuar struck him with a *lāthi* on a fatal spot. As the Pathan was dying he told Kuar that he must receive a little worship, and that he would take it by the side of Bir Kuar.

[1] Recorded in Milki and Uchaila.

THE ROLE OF THE GODLINGS 107

In the Babhantalao version this variant is carried over, but Kuar becomes the Ahirs generally and the Pathan obtains his worship by threatening to give constant trouble unless he is worshipped.

Finally, in a Jaintipur version, the Pathan becomes Gopi Mian, demands the milk when the *chhatia* is squatting on the pitchers and is struck dead by the *chhatia*.

The other forms in which the Muhammadan appears have either severely local myths or diffused but very summary ones, or they are simply names without legends. Thus the Muhammadan servant of the carpenter is said to have died through falling into a ditch while pursuing his master who was running to the scene of Birnath's death.[1] The Muhammadan friend and the Muhammadan cowherd die with Birnath in the jungle while protecting cattle.[2] Finally, the Khan Sahib, the dealer in bangles, the Jolaha and the anonymous Pathan are names and nothing else. Over them all move Gopi Mian[3] and Langru Bir, fastening their names first to one and then to another, but adding nothing to the actual origin of the Muhammadan stranger.

When we consider the various versions it is clear that the story of the landlord's servant is the more probable—it provides a credible starting-point for the worship—while the other variants are almost certainly substitute versions, developed when the memory of the incident was lost. But the incident seems scarcely the whole explanation, and if we are to understand why the Muhammadan is added we must look as well to the need which his presence serves.

This need arises from the heavily Muhammadan tone of the area with its Moghul traditions, its memories of Muhammadan power and continued presence of Muhammadans in the villages. Its total impact involves an effort of adjustment by the Ahirs which we may describe in terms of three needs—a need to assert Ahir superiority, a need to declare Ahir friendship and a need to appease Muhammadan violence. The strange Muhammadan who attends at Birnath's *pujā* and is given a minor offering is the means through which all these needs are satisfied. The substitute legends make him a Muhammadan friend and at the same time a Muhammadan servant--thus declaring Ahir friendship and Ahir superiority—while the offering to him as an individual acts also as a general appeasement.

[1] Muhammadganj.
[2] Khajuri.
[3] The name, Gopi Mian—meaning the Muhammadan with the Ahir functions—merely summarizes the situation.

108 THE VERTICAL MAN

The Muhammadan is present because in the circumstances of the area a *modus vivendi* with Muhammadans is necessary for the Ahir way of life.

III

THE BHUIYA

A similar effort of adjustment is represented in the offering to the Bhuiya. This occurs in villages in Fatehpur and Untari *thānās* and is represented by three different legends.

In the first the offering is to Tulsi Bir, the main caste deity of the Bhuiyas, who is said to have been a friend of Birnath.

In the second it is made to a Bhuiya, who is said to have killed Birnath for damaging his silk cocoons.

Finally, it is made to a Bhuiya named Madho Dank. According to this latter legend, Madho Dank was a friend of Basan Kuar (a substitute or pseudonym for Bir Kuar). After Bir Kuar's death, Basan Kuar decreed the death of Madho Dank, thinking that as they were not separated in life they should not be separated in death. He therefore caused Madho Dank to die and sent him in the form of a tiger to kill the Ahir's cattle. The ghost tiger killed some cattle. The Ahirs then began to worship both Basan Kuar and Madho Dank, and after this the ravages ceased.

We need not regard these legends as statements of historical truth, for their function is obvious. They act as an index to the local relations of Ahirs and Bhuiyas—in one case marred by friction and in the others marked by an equable ease. The extra offering is a symbol of all that Ahir-Bhuiya relations should be.

IV

THE SON, THE SERVANT AND THE PET

Finally, two other groups flit sporadically through the worship. They are firstly a nameless Rajput, and secondly a miscellaneous group covering a son, a servant and a pet.

In the rare villages where the Rajput receives a supplementary offering, the legends show him as a friend of Bir Kuar who was associated with his death. And just as the offerings to the Muhammadan and the Bhuiya express an inter-caste relation, we may see in these offerings also the expression of local Ahir-Rajput relations.

THE ROLE OF THE GODLINGS   109

In the case of the son, the servant and the pet, on the other hand, a caste relation is wanting and the offerings spring instead from inferences and assumptions. In the two villages where offerings are made to a son and a dog, the Ahirs do not say that Bir Kuar actually had a son and a dog. They say instead that as he was a truly bold Ahir he must have had them, and they interpret the deduction as a fact. The son and the pet, therefore, receive offerings because they are important appendixes of Bir Kuar rather than because they have any special roles.

A similar deduction explains the offering to the servant. In a few legends, the servant is a cowherd who is killed with Bir Kuar, and in these cases the joint death explains the joint offerings. But in many villages there is no legend and the servant ranges from a cowherd, a Jolaha, a Gorait, to a *begar* (or fag) and a body-guard. Here the Ahir's sense of Bir Kuar's greatness makes them attribute a servant to him, and the offerings are made to the servant partly as to a follower tinged with Bir Kuar's divinity but partly with the idea of having their main offerings recommended. Just as Roman Catholics regard saints as go-betweens between themselves and God, the Ahirs reinforce their offerings to Bir Kuar by placating his servant. The servants, in fact, owe their mysterious presence in the worship to the Ahir sense of Bir Kuar's might.

THE CONTROL OF TIGERS

In the legends which I have given in the text, Bir Kuar is often assailed by tigers, and it is through a tigress that he ultimately meets his death. It is this method of death, the fact that the tigress is the death agent, which partially accounts for one of his minor functions—the protection of the herds from the ravages of tigers.

Throughout the Bir Kuar country, a man who is killed by a tiger is worshipped as a *baghaut*, "one who has taken the tiger on him" and has thus become an oblation for his fellows. The experience of this kind of death enables him, as it were, to control the death agent, and it is through the *baghaut* that Ahirs and others win temporary immunity in tiger-infested country. Bir Kuar, being also a *baghaut*, has also this power of controlling tigers, and it will illustrate this minor role if I record another *chānchar* from the same region. In this ballad Madhumalati is only nominally the heroine, for the object of the ballad, as the final lines make clear, is to glorify yet again the power of Bir Kuar to subjugate tigers, and to demonstrate his dominion.

29

Daughter of a raja was Madhumalati
And she goes for pilgrimage to Kashi Pareyag
To Kashi Pareyag she goes for pilgrimage
The Moghul soldiers have pitched their tents
Madhumalati sees the camp
And bitterly Madhumalati weeps
There is none of my village neither friend nor enemy
How shall I send a message home?
Weeping, weeping her eyes
Swell to a red flower
And her *sāri* is wet with wiping the tears
Up in the sky circles a female vulture
"Vulture, my aunt are you
At home I have left the mother of my sins
Oh! be to me a mother of goodness
Why did I start for Kashi Pareyag on pilgrimage?
The Moghuls are in camp
There is none of my village neither friend nor enemy
How can I send a message home?
The mother of my sins
Why did I leave at home?

THE CONTROL OF TIGERS

III

O my aunt
Be to me a mother of goodness
Carry a message to my father
And my father will tell Tulsi my brother
And Tulsi will tell my husband
And my husband will save me from the Moghuls."
Answers the vulture
"Listen, my daughter. I am only a vulture
How should a vulture carry news?"
Madhumalati tears her *sari*
And the pencilled black of her eyes she uses as ink
And she trims her nail to a quill
And she traces her story in a letter[1]
Giving details of her state
And the agony of her heart
Finished Madhumalati sends the letter
And the vulture takes it in her talons
Speeding to her father's house
And her father's court
And drops the letter from the sky
Madhumalati's father gets the letter
And dismayed he learns its message
Then he tells her brother Tulsi
Tulsi gets ready at once
And the three start with the army
Her father moves on the royal elephant
Her brother rides his charger
Her husband goes on a fighting tiger
And they join battle with the Moghuls
But the Moghuls batter and rout them
Then Madhumalati speaks
"Listen, O Moghul Pathan
The chief elephant, give back to my father

[1] There is a parallel situation in the Chhattisgarh song, "The Story of Dhola."
"Princess, I am here to serve you. Tell me what I can do for you.
Of what can I make paper and what shall I use for ink?
What pen can I use to write a word or two of love?"
"For paper tear your *sari*, take the lamp black from your eyes
For a pen use your little finger to write a word or two of love."
Maru tears her precious *sari*, she takes the lamp black from her eyes.
With her little finger she writes a word or two of love.

(Verrier Elwin, op. cit., 378–379)

THE VERTICAL MAN

The dappled charger, give back to my brother
And some marriage trinkets give to my husband
To marry again a girl of his caste."
The Moghul
Gives to her father the elephant
Gives to her brother the dappled charger
Gives to her husband the marriage trinkets
To marry a girl of his caste
Again Madhumalati speaks
"Listen, O Moghul Pathan
Bring a litter with a million diamonds
And a southern *sari*
And thirty-two bearers
And I start for your home."
The Moghul brings
A litter with a million diamonds
And a southern *sari*
And thirty-two bearers
And they start for his home.
Scarcely are they gone than Baba Birnath appears
He sends a tiger
Quickly it widows Madhumalati
While Birnath gathers the travelling litter
And brings it to his fort.
On the roof is Madhumalati's mother
"O Madhumalati
You have saved the honour of the house
The honour of two families is saved."

BIBLIOGRAPHICAL NOTES

(1) FRANCIS BUCHANAN. *Shahabad Journal*, 1812–13, edited by C. E. A.W. Oldham (Patna, Bihar, 1926). Contains vivid notes on the Sasaram landscape, the habits of Ahirs, and on the stone-cutting trade carried on by Gonrs. In a list of village gods, a solitary reference is made to Bir Kuar under the spelling "Vir Kungar." There are unfortunately no notes either on the images or the cult.

(2) H. H. RISLEY. *The Tribes and Castes of Bengal* (Calcutta, 1891). The article on Goala gives a survey of the Ahir caste in Bengal and Bihar, but the list of sub-castes is inaccurate and incomplete. There is a reference to the dance of the cows but not to Bir Kuar.

(3) W. CROOKE. *The Tribes and Castes of the North-Western Provinces and Oudh* (Calcutta, 1896) Gives a note on Birnath and refers to the dance of the cows. It is doubtful whether many of the statements are strictly accurate, and there is no evidence which in any way connects Birnath with the Bangarama quintette (page 64).

(4) L. S. S. O'MALLEY. *Bengal District Gazetteers; Palamau* (Calcutta, 1907). Gives a largely inaccurate account of the Bir Kuar cult and confuses it with the Bir Puja of Bhuiyas.

(5) L. S. S. O'MALLEY. *Bihar and Orissa District Gazetteers; Patna.* Revised edition by J. F. W. James (Patna, 1924). Pages 51–52 give a summary account of the *gai dārh*.

(6) W. CROOKE. *Religion and Folklore of Northern India* (Oxford, 1926). Contains two references to Bir Kuar. Page 132 states that "in the United Provinces Ahirs worship Birnath, 'hero lord,' who is said to be a man of the caste who was killed by a tiger and now protects their cattle in the jungle," while page 325 notes that "Birnath, the Ahir cattle godling, is represented by a post." A poor copy of such a post, obviously artificially commissioned, was presented by Crooke to the Pitt-Rivers Museum, Oxford, where it is labelled "an Ahir fetish."

(7) SARAT CHANDRA MITRA. "On the cult of the godling Bir Kuar in the Palamau District in Chota Nagpur," *Journal of the Bihar and Orissa Research Society*, March–June 1938. Analyses the accounts of Bir Kuar given in 4 and offers an interesting commentary. As, however, almost all the facts in 4 are wrong, little of the commentary is valid.

THE VERTICAL MAN

(8) RAM NARESH TRIPATHI. *Kabita Kaumudi. Part V Gram Git* (Hindi Mandir, Allahabad, 1929). The first big collection of Hindi folk-songs (including Ahir) to be published in India and as a pioneer effort deserving of the highest praise. The songs number 275 and are selected from a much larger collection made in the eastern districts of the United Provinces and the western districts of Bihar. The songs are grouped according to the occasions on which they are sung, but there is no note of the castes or areas from which they were collected.

GLOSSARY

Achhat: Rice from paddy which has not been boiled (*arwa chāwal*); as distinct from rice from paddy which has been half-boiled before being threshed (*usina chāwal*).

Akhāra: A dancing floor.

Babur: A thorny tree, *Acacia arabica.*

Baghaut: A man killed by a tiger.

Bakauthi: A religious bargain by which supernatural help is given in return for worship or sacrifice.

Balua: An axe shaped like a halberd.

Bansula: A carpenter's adze.

Barua: A divine steed on which a god or goddess rides.

Bathan: The place where buffaloes are tethered.

Begar: A person forced to do unpaid labour.

Bel: A tree, *Aegle marmelos.*

Bhang: A narcotic preparation made from the leaves of a sister plant to *gānjā, Canabis sativa.* The sprigs of dried leaves are powdered and made up into a drink by mixing them with almonds, sugar, milk and water. It is said to give a feeling of hilarity and elation. "You feel as if you are flying through the air."

Bhatua: A vegetable like a marrow.

Birahā: A verse form.

Chabutra: A mud platform.

Chamār: A skinner or tanner.

Chānchar: A verse form.

Chauka: A square marked out with powdered rice.

Chaurā: A *chabutra* or mud platform.

Chhān: The rope for tethering or hobbling buffaloes.

Chhatia: A medium.

Chilam: An earthenware pipe which swells out into a small saucer, used for smoking.

Dhenuā: A mythical cow that gives milk all the year round.

Dhoti: A length of cloth used for draping a man's waist.

Dihwar: The watchman god.

Dohā: A verse form.

Gai dārh: The dance of the cows.

Gānjā: A narcotic preparation made from the dried flowers of a tall bushy plant, *Canabis indica,* with flowers like a French marigold. The dried flowers are crushed and mixed with tobacco in equal parts. The mixed pellet of *gānjā* and tobacco is then put in a *chilam.* A lighted coal is added and the smoke inhaled. It is said to induce, at first, a feeling of energy, but later a kind of mad blankness.

Gaunā: The ceremony of the second marriage, or installation of the bride in the husband's house.

Ghi: Clarified butter, like white tallow.

THE VERTICAL MAN

Gur: Country sugar.
Guru: A spiritual teacher.
Haldi: Turmeric.
Hansua: A large sickle.
Hum: Incense made from setting fire to *ghi* poured on straw.
Khel: Literally "play" but here with the special meaning of "possession."
Khir: A kind of milk pudding made with rice, milk, sugar and *ghi*.
Lāthi: A long wooden stave.
Laung kā chhak: Cardamon water offered to a god.
Lorikāin: The ballad of Lorik.
Lotā: A brass water pot.
Mahuā: Bassia latifolia.
Mantrā: A religious incantation.
Otā: A mud platform.
Pahardār: A body-guard.
Pakka: Well-made. A macadamized road is a *pakka* road.
Palki: A palanquin.
Pān: A mixture of lime and areca nut, folded inside a betel leaf and chewed
   like tobacco.
Pāwā: A quarter of a seer.
Pie: A small copper coin, value about a farthing.
Pujā: A religious ceremony or worship.
Puri: A mixture of flour, water and *ghi*, fried in *ghi*.
Roti: Indian bread made from water and flour and baked dry.
Sadhu: A religious mendicant.
Sadr Subdivision: The headquarters subdivision of a district.
Sakhi: A girl friend.
Sāmbar: A form of deer, *Cervus unicoler.*
Sāri: A length of cloth draped to form a woman's dress.
Sati: A woman who commits *sati*, i.e. who of her own free will burns on her
   husband's funeral pyre.
Tapāwan: Liquor offered to a god.
Thānā: A police station or unit of police administration.
Thekua: A thick slab of wheat powder mixed with *gur* and fried in *ghi*.
Tola: A hamlet.

LIST OF VILLAGES

Village	*Police Station*	*District*
Amahua	Rohtas	Shahabad
Amba	Hariharganj	Palamau
Ananditchak	Rohtas	Shahabad
Ararua Kalan	Hariharganj	Palamau
Arjundih	Chhatarpur	Palamau
Babhandi	Chhatarpur	Palamau
Bagen	Dehri	Shahabad
Bahera	Sasaram	Shahabad
Bahiar Khurd	Untari	Palamau
Bajnia	Barun	Gaya
Baknaur	Rohtas	Shahabad
Bank	Dehri	Shahabad
Bankheta	Bhaunathpur	Palamau
Banua	Rohtas	Shahabad
Banwari	Bhaunathpur	Palamau
Bara	Chhatarpur	Palamau
Baradih	Sasaram	Shahabad
Barahi	Hussainabad	Gaya
Baraiya	Chhatarpur	Palamau
Barka Tiara	Rohtas	Shahabad
Basant Bigha	Nabinagar	Gaya
Basaura	Nabinagar	Gaya
Baskatia	Rohtas	Shahabad
Belanja	Barun	Gaya
Benibigha	Nabinagar	Gaya
Bhadsa	Rohtas	Shahabad
Bhisra	Rohtas	Shahabad
Bishunpur	Rohtas	Shahabad
Chacharia	Bhaunathpur	Palamau
Chachayia	Bhaunathpur	Palamau
Chakandhawa	Dehri	Shahabad
Chakla Makritola	Bhaunathpur	Palamau
Chandanpura	Sasaram	Shahabad
Chandargarh	Nabinagar	Gaya
Chapra	Dehri	Shahabad
Chatra	Aurangabad	Gaya
Churesar	Rohtas	Shahabad
Dadara Pokrahi	Hussainabad	Palamau
Dangwar	Hussainabad	Palamau

Darahi	Hussainabad	Palamau
Daranagar (Turki tola)	Rohtas	Shahabad
Deuria	Dehri	Shahabad
Dhoba	Fatehpur	Gaya
Dinadag	Chhatarpur	Palamau
Gauhara	Hariharganj	Palamau
Ghuna Bigha	Rohtas	Shahabad
Gondaria (Bahera tola)	Chatra	Hazaribagh
Goradih	Leslieganj	Palamau
Gotha	Chhatarpur	Palamau
Hardaspur	Sherghati	Gaya
Hariharganj	Hariharganj	Palamau
Hisag	Chhatarpur	Palamau
Indrapura	Sasaram	Shahabad
Jaintipur	Rohtas	Shahabad
Jairagi	Chainpur	Ranchi
Jamuni	Daltonganj	Palamau
Kalapahar	Chhatarpur	Palamau
Kanker	Nabinagar	Gaya
Karma Bairia tola	Chhatarpur	Palamau
Katar	Dehri	Shahabad
Kauwal	Chhatarpur	Palamau
Khaira	Nabinagar	Gaya
Khajuri	Rohtas	Shahabad
Kharwardih	Chhatarpur	Palamau
Khatin	Chhatarpur	Palamau
Koeridih	Nabinagar	Gaya
Kundari	Leslieganj	Palamau
Kurasin	Sherghati	Gaya
Kurd	Rohtas	Shahabad
Kusahar	Chhatarpur	Palamau
Kusiara	Hussainabad	Palamau
Lahanga	Chhatarpur	Palamau
Lakhea	Garhwa	Palamau
Lateya	Chhatarpur	Palamau
Lawadag	Chhatarpur	Palamau
Longraha	Hariharganj	Palamau
Madhkupia	Rohtas	Shahabad
Madhurampur	Dehri	Shahabad

LIST OF VILLAGES

Maharajganj	Sasaram	Shahabad
Mahauli	Dudhi	Mirzapur
Mahesara	Chhatarpur	Palamau
Majhiyawan	Nabinagar	Gaya
Mali	Nabinagar	Gaya
Mananpur	Chhatarpur	Palamau
Manhania	Sasaram	Shahabad
Mathurapur	Dehri	Shahabad
Milki	Rohtas	Shahabad
Mirsarae	Sasaram	Shahabad
Muhammadganj	Hussainabad	Palamau
Narari	Barun	Gaya
Nawadih	Rohtas	Shahabad
Nayagaon	Rohtas	Shahabad
Naykagaon	Rohtas	Shahabad
Nimahat	Rohtas	Shahabad
Nishunpur	Rohtas	Shahabad
Paharia	Rohtas	Shahabad
Pandaria	Bhaunathpur	Palamau
Panha	Hazaribagh	Hazaribagh
Parcha	Rohtas	Shahabad
Parha	Kutumba	Gaya
Pipardih	Aurangabad	Gaya
Purnadih	Rohtas	Shahabad
Rambandh	Hussainabad	Palamau
Ramdihra	Rohtas	Shahabad
Ramgarh	Chhatarpur	Palamau
Ramna	Untari	Palamau
Ranjitganj	Rohtas	Shahabad
Rohtas (Bhabhantalao)	Rohtas	Shahabad
Rohtas (Bholna tola)	Rohtas	Shahabad
Rohtas Kila	Rohtas	Shahabad
Rudwa	Chhatarpur	Palamau
Sahaspur	Barun	Gaya
Samauta	Rohtas	Shahabad
Saraiya	Rohtas	Shahabad
Sarma (Tenudih tola)	Chhatarpur	Palamau
Selupara	Madanpur	Palamau
Shankarpur	Dehri	Shahabad
Sheikhpura	Barun	Gaya
Simarbari	Hariharganj	Palamau
Siris	Barun	Gaya
Sitalpur	Fatehpur	Gaya

THE VERTICAL MAN

Sonbarsa	Hussainabad	Palamau
Sunri	Panki	Palamau
Tardih	Rohtas	Shahabad
Tendua (Ratanpura tola)	Nabinagar	Gaya
Tenua Dusadhi	Dehri	Shahabad
Tiara	Rohtas	Shahabad
Tilauthu	Sasaram	Shahabad
Tilokhar	Rohtas	Shahabad
Tipa	Rohtas	Shahabad
Tumba	Rohtas	Shahabad
Turki	Rohtas	Shahabad
Uchaila	Rohtas	Shahabad
Uchaili	Madanpur	Palamau
Urdana	Nabinagar	Gaya

INDEX

Ahirs, 17, 25–7, 31–2, 35–8, 48–9, 62, 79–80, 82, 84–5, 87, 91, 93–5, 105–9
Archer, Mildred, 15, 18
Auden, W. H., 5, 44
Azfar, M., 15

Barhi, Bishuni, Baldeo and Thakuri, wood carvers, 89
Barhis, 13, 87, 89–90, 92–6
Bhattacharjee, N. L., 15
Bhuiya, 33, 34, 108
Birkhod, Rajput, Kayasth and Brahman death ceremony, 82
Birnath, *see* Bir Kuar
Bir Kuar:
  cattle god, 17, 25–6, 48, 81–2, 91–2
  songs of praise, 27–31
  wife, 50–1, 58, 62, 65, 68, 70, 95–6, 78, 80, 99
  sister, 52–3, 54–6, 60–72, 74, 76, 78, 80, 99
  and the carpenter, 62, 83–4
  other relatives, 56–8, 60, 99–100
  relationship with Krishna, 99–104
  identification with the lame man, 105–6
  son, 108–9
  and Madhumalati, 110–12
Bir Kuar, the myth:
  rudimentary forms, 49–52
  substitute legends, 51
  main myth, 53, 70–81
  witch motif, 53–61, 71, 74, 77–9
  Parai the buffalo, 56–60, 63–5, 67, 71, 73–5, 78–9, 80
  brother-sister motif, 60–70, 80
  Banda and Barowa, buffaloes, 62
  the fertilizer god, 80
  the model, 80
  the lesson, 81
Bir Kuar, ritual:
  Sohrai festival, 26–7, 31–2, 36–41, 99
  Diwali night, 31
  minor figures worshipped, 32–5
  bakauthi (or bargain), 36
  answer to the prayer, 37–8
  purchase of goat, 38

Bir Kuar, ritual—*continued*
  summoning of the medium, 38
  boiling of the milk, 39
  goat sacrifice, 39–41
  medium's ecstacy, 41
  pantomime of the tiger, 41
  pantomime of the lame man, 41–2
  pantomime of the horse, 43
  termination of extended worship, 43
  clay horses, 44
  installation of images, 44–5
  dance of the cows, 45–7
Broom, in magic, 55
Buchanan, Francis, 113
Buffaloes, 25, 36–7, 48, 77–80, 91
  buffalo obsession, 81
  see also Bir Kuar myth

Carpenter, *see* Bir Kuar myth
Celtic sculpture, 14
Chanchars, 49, 60, 65, 68, 70, 73, 75
Clay horses, 44
Crooke, W., 113

Dance of the cows, 45–7
De Zoete, Beryl, 15
Dehon, P., 55
Diwali night, 31
Dog, the, 108–9

Early English sculpture, 13
Ellis, Havelock, 61
Elwin, Verrier, 55, 69, 75, 111

Fertilizer god, *see* Bir Kuar myth
Folk-songs of Chhattisgarh, 69, 75, 111
Frankish-Alemannic ivory, 92
Fumet, D. V., 5

Geometric art, 18–19
Gonr:
  Aklu and Mahangu Gonr, stone carvers, 88, 92
  Ram Charitra and Ram Prasad Gonr, stone carvers, 88
Gonrs, 13, 87–9, 92–6
Gopi, Mian, 34, 35, 106–7
Grierson, Sir George, 58

122 THE VERTICAL MAN

Grimm's *Teutonic Mythology*, 58
Grove, marriage of, 82

Helion, paintings by, 18
Hutton, J. H., 45–6

Installation of images, 44–5

Kani Biramdeia, 53
Krishna, 26–7, 99–104

Lakshmi, 31
Langru Bir, the lame man, 32, 33, 105–6 *see also* Bir Kuar myth

MacNeice, Louise, 24
Madho Dank, 108
Madhumalati ballad, 110–12
Malik, M. I., 15
Mediums, 38–9, 41–2, 104–6
Mitra, Sarat Chandra, 113
Moore, Henry, 19
Muhammadan, the strange, 106–8 *see also* Bir Kuar myth

Negro sculpture, 14
Nicholson, Ben, 18

Ocean of Love, The, 104
Ocean of Story, The, 58–9
Old Lay of Gudrun, The, 58
O'Malley, L. S. S., 82, 113

Parai, the pet buffalo, *see* Bir Kuar myth
Peck, N. F., 14
Penzer, N. M., 58–9
Phillpotts, Bertha S., 58
Picasso, 91
Piper, John, 13
Pollard, A. W., 30–1
Prasad, Sadashwa, 15
Prasad, Sankta, 15
Prideaux, C. T., 15

Rajput, the nameless, 33, 108–9

Read, Herbert, 13, 18
Risley, H. H., 113
Rousseau, 36
Russell, R. V., and Hiralal, 56, 84

Sabharwal, L. R., 15
Salome, 30
Santal painting, 18
Sculpture:
stone and wooden images, 17, 20–4, 48
muscular guardian type, 23
benign hero type, 23
doomed tough type, 24
installation of, 44–5
parallels, 82–4
origin of features, 84
causes of wooden sculpture, 84–5
development of stone sculpture, 85
restriction of stone sculpture, 86
regional styles, 87–90
process of stone carving, 88–90
process of wood carving, 89–90
economics of carving, 92–4
Sheikh Babal, 35, 62
Sohrai, *see* Bir Kuar ritual
Son river, 17, 86
Stone images, *see* Sculpture
Stone quarries, 85–6

Tennis, 31
Tigers, 17, 110–12, *see also* Bir Kuar myth
Tools, 88
Tripathi, Ram Naresh, 114

Vertical man, 5
Viswa Karma, 34
legend, 83–4
Vital geometry, 18–24, 92, 95–6

Well, marriage of, 82
Witchcraft, 52–9, *see also* Bir Kuar myth
Wooden images, *see* Sculpture
Worringer, Wilhelm, 18–19, 92